Study

Lifespan Human Development

FOURTH EDITION

Anne V. Gormly
David M. Brodzinsky

Prepared by Carolyn D. Smith

Holt, Rinehart and Winston, Inc.
Fort Worth   Chicago   San Francisco   Philadelphia
Montreal   Toronto   London   Sydney
Tokyo

ISBN 0-03-025394-2

Printed in the United States of America
  0 1 2 018 9 8 7 6 5 4 3

Holt, Rinehart and Winston, Inc.
The Dryden Press
Saunders College Publishing

PREFACE

This study guide is designed to accompany *Lifespan Human Development*, by Anne V. Gormly and David M. Brodzinsky. It can be used to review each chapter in the text or as a study aid in preparing for tests. Each chapter of the guide corresponds to a chapter of the text and is divided into the following sections: (1) Chapter Outline, (2) Summary of Key Concepts, (3) Key Terms and Phrases, (4) Review Questions, (5) Exercises, and (6) Quiz.

Chapter Outline: This brief outline will help you recall the main topics covered in the chapter.

Summary of Key Concepts: Read this section and think about it before continuing your review. It will help you focus on the major concepts discussed in the chapter.

Key Terms and Phrases: This section lists the terms that appear in boldface type in the text. If you are not familiar with a term or phrase, review the section of the chapter in which it is presented.

Review Questions: These questions ask you to recall in general terms the most important topics discussed in the chapter.

Exercises: These ask you to list or chart important information presented in the chapter. They will help you review stages of development, compare theories, and check your understanding of multidimensional concepts.

Quiz: This section enables you to review the chapter in detail. It includes true-false, sentence completion, multiple-choice, and matching items. The questions in each subsection are presented in the order in which they appear in the text. Use the quiz to test yourself; the answers are presented at the end of the chapter. If you find that you have answered an item incorrectly, review the section of the chapter in which it is presented.

The purpose of this study guide is to help you learn the material presented in *Lifespan Human Development*. It is not intended to serve as a substitute for the text. The best way to use this guide is as follows:

1. Read a chapter in the text carefully, noting the key words and concepts presented.

2. Work through the corresponding chapter in the guide, including the quiz.

3. Go back to the text to review areas in which your grasp of the subject matter is weak.

The more careful and thorough you are in following these steps, the better your learning and test performance will be.

TABLE OF CONTENTS

Chapter 1

LIFESPAN DEVELOPMENT:
ISSUES, THEORIES, AND METHODS

CHAPTER OUTLINE

Lifespan Approach
The Study of Human Development
    Determinants of Development
    The Role of Theory
Major Contemporary Theories: An Introduction
    Psychoanalytic Theories
        Freud: Psychosexual Development
        Erikson: Psychosocial Development
    Cognitive Theories
        Piaget: Cognitive Development
        Information-Processing Theories
    Behavioral Theories
        Pavlov: Classical Conditioning
        Skinner: Operant Conditioning
        Social-Learning Theory
Methods of Studying Development
    Research Designs
        Cross-Sectional Design
        Longitudinal Design
    Data-Collection Techniques
        Interview Techniques
        Observational Techniques
        Experimental Techniques
        Standardized Tests
    Issues in Data Collection
        Sampling
        Reliability and Validity
        Choosing a Research Strategy
    Ethical Considerations in Research

SUMMARY OF KEY CONCEPTS

1. *Developmental psychology* focuses on the changes that normally occur in body, thought, emotions, and behavior over the course of a lifespan. Issues that are of particular concern to lifespan researchers are the cumulative effects of changes across the lifespan, the overall contexts in which change occurs, and the degree of change that can occur at any age.

2. The question of what determines development is one of the oldest controversies in recorded history. In contemporary times the controversy has centered on two

major factors: *heredity* (the genetic program that is passed along from parents to offspring at the time of conception) and *environment* (the vast array of experiences to which the individual is exposed from the time of conception until death).

3. A *theory* is a set of coherent interrelated statements, laws, and principles that describe, define, and predict specific aspects of some phenomenon such as human behavioral development. Theories both describe phenomena and set limits on them; they also generate new ideas for research and bring together existing data into an integrated and logically consistent system.

4. Psychoanalytic theories of development are concerned primarily with the personality and emotional development of individuals. Freud's theory of psychosexual development described development as a series of stages in which the individual must learn how to express specific sexual and aggressive instincts in a way that is acceptable both to the self and to society. Erikson's theory of psychosocial development describes a series of crises that occur in response to demands that society places on the developing individual to conform to adult expectations about self-expression and self-reliance.

5. *Cognitive development* refers to the orderly changes that occur in the way people intellectually understand and cope with their world. Piaget's theory of cognitive development describes several stages of mental reasoning; at each stage the child "constructs" knowledge differently. Information-processing theory, in contrast, describes how people receive, represent, and process information; in this view, the basic processes for performing these tasks do not change with age, but their capacity, efficiency, and speed improve.

6. The behavioral approach explains human development as the accumulated effects of learning, either through conditioning or through social processes. In *classical conditioning*, an automatic involuntary response comes to be associated with a new stimulus that does not normally elicit such a response. *Operant conditioning* is based on the principle that a behavior that produces a pleasant or rewarding consequence for the learner is likely to be repeated. Social-learning theory emphasizes such processes as imitation of models such as parents and peers.

7. To conduct a research study, the investigator must first define the specific question or problem to be explored. Once the problem is defined, it must be reformulated into a statement about the relationship between two or more *variables*. The variables, in turn, must be *operationalized*, that is, clearly defined in ways that will allow the researcher to observe and measure them.

8. The two basic research designs are cross sectional and longitudinal. In *cross-sectional research*, individuals of different ages are tested or observed at the same point in time. *Longitudinal research* involves repeatedly testing the same group of individuals over a period of time.

9. The techniques used by researchers to collect data include interview techniques, observational techniques, experimental techniques, and standardized tests. Among the issues that must be addressed in collecting data are the selection of

a representative sample; the *reliability* or consistency of the technique used (i.e., whether it obtains the same results each time it measures the same phenomena); and *validity*, or the extent to which a test or scale measures what it is supposed to measure.

10. In planning a research project, one of the most important things the investigator must keep in mind is the potential effect on the subjects participating in the experiment.

KEY TERMS AND PHRASES

developmental psychology
theory
id — *OUR MOST BASIC BIOLOG. & EMOT, URGES*
superego — *CONSCIENCE & MORAL VALUES*   [FREUD]
ego — *PART OF SYSTEM RESPONSIBLE FOR REALISTIC ADAPTATION TO WORLD*
cognitive development — *CHANGES IN VARIETY OF INTELLECTUAL DEVELOP.*
constructivism
symbol
sensorimotor stage — *1st STAGE OF COGNITIVE DEV (INFANT)*
preoperational thought — *2nd " " " " (AGE 2-6)—NO LOGIC*   [PIAGET]
concrete operations — *3rd " " " " (LOGIC & SYMBOLS)*
formal operations — *4th " " " " (ADOLESCEN + — LOGIC, ABSTRACT, HYPOTHETICAL)*
information-processing theory
reinforcement
social-learning theory
cross-sectional research
cohort
longitudinal research
interview techniques
observational techniques
experimental techniques
standardized test
random selection
reliability
validity

REVIEW QUESTIONS

1. What is developmental psychology? What is meant by the lifespan approach to development?

2. What are the basic determinants of development?

3. What is a theory? What are the four basic functions of theories?

4. What are the three major theoretical approaches to understanding human development?

5. How does cross-sectional research differ from longitudinal research?

6. List the advantages and disadvantages of the four basic data collection techniques.

7. What is meant by random selection, reliability, and validity?

8. Why are ethical considerations important in designing a research study?

EXERCISES

1. Compare Freud and Erikson's stages of psychosexual and psychosocial development.

AGE	FREUD	ERIKSON
Birth-1.5 years		
1.5-3 years		
3-6 years		
6-12 years		
12-18 years		
Young adulthood		
Middle adulthood		

Older adulthood

2. Describe the stages in Piaget's theory of cognitive development.

AGE	STAGE	FOCUS
Birth-1.5 years	SENSORIMOTOR	
1.5-3 years	PREOPERATION	
3-6 years		
6-12 years	CONCRETE	
12-18 years	FORMAL	

QUIZ

True or False

__F__ 1. Developmental psychology is an ancient discipline that has its roots in Aristotelian philosophy.

__F__ 2. The lifespan approach to the study of human development is concerned with development from birth to adulthood.

__F__ 3. The research of developmental psychologists is "pure" rather than "applied" or practical.

__T__ 4. Heredity refers to the genetic program that is passed from parents to offspring at the time of conception.

__T__ 5. Neither heredity nor environment alone can adequately explain the way in which human beings develop.

__F__ 6. The main function of a theory is to operationalize variables so that they can be observed and measured.

__T__ 7. Psychoanalytic theories of development focus on the way in which people's emotional and biological needs adapt to the requirements of the society in which they live.

T 8. In Freud's theory of psychosexual development, the first stage is the oral stage.

F 9. In Freud's model of the personality, the ego is the most primitive part of the personality and is present at birth.

F 10. According to Erikson, the final psychosocial crisis occurs in adolescence.

T 11. According to the philosophical perspective known as constructivism, all that we know of reality is based on our mental constructions or ideas.

F 12. The Swiss psychologist Jean Piaget was the originator of information-processing theory.

T 13. The final stage of cognitive development in Piaget's theory is the stage of formal operations.

T 14. In the early years of life memory is mostly involuntary.

F 15. Classical conditioning is based on the principle that a behavior that produces a rewarding consequence for the learner will be repeated.

T 16. Much of what we know about operant conditioning is a result of research by B. F. Skinner.

F 17. According to social-learning theory, responses cannot be acquired without exposure to direct reinforcement.

F 18. The first step in designing a research study is to select a method for collecting data.

T 19. In cross-sectional research, individuals of different ages are tested or observed at the same point in time.

T 20. Longitudinal research involves large investments of time and money.

T 21. Interview techniques usually involve one-on-one interchanges between the subject and the investigator.

F 22. Observational techniques are especially well suited to studying behaviors that occur infrequently, such as altruism.

F 23. Reliability refers to the extent to which a test or scale measures what it is supposed to measure.

T 24. The choice of a research strategy is closely tied to the investigator's theoretical orientation.

F 25. Research with subjects who are relatively powerless does not pose potential ethical problems for the researcher.

Sentence Completion

1. A focus on _CHANGE_ is what makes developmental psychology unique.

2. The research of developmental psychologists has a practical application for the formulation of _SOCIAL POLICY_

3. _____ refers to the vast array of experiences to which the individual is exposed from the time of conception until death.

4. The controversy over what determines development centers on two major factors: _____ and _____.

5. A _____ is a set of coherent interrelated statements, laws, and principles.

6. Some developmental theories view human beings as basically _____ while others view them as inherently _____.

7. The three major theoretical perspectives on development are _____ theory, _____ theory, and _____ theory.

8. In Freud's theory, the stage of psychosexual development occurring between the ages of 3 and 6 is the _____ stage.

9. In Erikson's theory, the stage of oral gratification is also the stage at which the infant establishes _TRUST_ in the nurturing figure.

10. Thinking, problem solving, and memory are examples of _COGNITIVE_ processes.

11. In Piaget's theory, the first stage of cognitive development is the _SENSORI MOTOR_ stage.

12. Piaget used the term _FORMAL OPERATIONS_ to refer to what we usually call abstract thought.

13. The flow of information begins with some sort of _____, which is processed in various ways and eventually leads to some sort of _____.

14. _____ memory is present even in young infants and appears not to change very much across the lifespan.

15. Two strategies that are effective in helping people remember things are _____ and _____.

16. The first laws of learning were established by the Russian physiologist _PAVLOV_.

17. A specially designed box used in operant conditioning is known as a _SKINNER BOX_.

18. According to social-learning theory, much of what children learn occurs through their natural tendency to _IMITATE_ the behavior of others.

19. Theories are usually stated in rather _BROAD_ and _GEN'L_ terms.

7

20. Once a research problem has been defined, it must be reformulated into a statement about the relationship between two or more _____.

21. A _Cohort_ is a group of individuals born during the same period.

22. _____ techniques record the ongoing behavior of individuals with as little interaction as possible between observer and subjects.

23. In experimental research, the investigator manipulates one set of variables--called the _____ variables--and observes their influence on another set of variables--the _____ variables.

24. The Minnesota Multiphasic Personality Inventory is an example of a _____.

25. Researchers frequently use the principles of _____ to ensure that every member of the population being studied has the same chance of being chosen for the study.

Multiple Choice

_C_ 1.　Developmental psychology is concerned with
　　　a.　the way memory operates.
　　　b.　the nature of human interaction.
　　　c.　the changes that occur over the course of a lifespan.
　　　d.　the biological differences between people of different ages.

_B_ 2.　Which of the following statements is *not* true?
　　　a.　Each human being is a unique individual.
　　　b.　The question of what determines development became a subject of heated debate in the 1960s.
　　　c.　Heredity refers to the genetic program that is passed along from parents to offspring.
　　　d.　Contemporary investigators believe that development must be understood in terms of the interaction between heredity and the environment.

_C_ 3.　Which of the following is *not* an environmental factor affecting human development?
　　　a.　exposure to disease or drugs
　　　b.　inadequate nutrition
　　　c.　the individual's genetic makeup
　　　d.　interactions within the family

_D_ 4.　Theories serve which of the following functions?
　　　a.　descriptive
　　　b.　generative
　　　c.　integrative
　　　d.　all of the above

A 5. Theorists who believe that development is best thought of as a continuous process focus on
   a. quantitative change in the individual.
   b. qualitative differences between individuals.
   c. human beings as passive and reactive.
   d. human beings as inherently active.

C 6. In which stage of Freud's theory of psychosexual development is sexual gratification based on true intimacy?
   a. oral
   b. phallic
   c. genital
   d. none of the above

D 7. In Freud's model of the personality, the standards, values, and mores of society are represented in the form of the
   a. id.
   b. ego.
   c. superid.
   d. superego.

A 8. Which of the following developed a theory in which a series of crises occur in response to demands that society places on the developing individual?
   a. Erik Erikson
   b. Jean Piaget
   c. Ann Brown
   d. Ivan Pavlov

B 9. The belief that our knowledge of reality is a function of the particular system of mental rules by which we organize information is known as
   a. formal operations.
   b. constructivism.
   c. information-processing theory.
   d. random selection.

A 10. In the stage of cognitive development known as preoperational thought, children are able to
   a. use symbol systems to represent the objects and events they experience.
   b. think about how things change from one state to another.
   c. reason about things that have no concrete existence.
   d. none of the above.

B 11. In which stage of cognitive development do children become capable of thinking about how things change?
   a. formal operations
   b. concrete operations
   c. the preoperational stage
   d. the sensorimotor stage

_D_ 12. In the stage of cognitive development known as formal operations, adolescents are able to
  a. represent transformations mentally.
  b. think about hypothetical events.
  c. reason about ideals and philosophy.
  d. all of the above.

_C_ 13. Information-processing theory has had its greatest impact on our understanding of
  a. conditioning.
  b. sensory experience.
  c. memory.
  d. social learning.

_A_ 14. The behavioral approach explains human development as the accumulated effects of
  a. learning.
  b. heredity.
  c. physical maturation.
  d. changes in the personality.

_B_ 15. Any stimulus that follows a behavior and results in that behavior being repeated is a
  a. conditioner.
  b. reinforcement.
  c. model.
  d. symbol.

_D_ 16. A leading proponent of social-learning theory is
  a. Ivan Pavlov.
  b. B. F. Skinner.
  c. Jean Piaget.
  d. Albert Bandura.

_C_ 17. According to social-learning theory, responses can be acquired without direct exposure to direct
  a. conditioning.
  b. modeling.
  c. reinforcement.
  d. punishment.

_B_ 18. The first step in designing a research study is
  a. operationalizing the variables.
  b. defining the problem.
  c. selecting the sample.
  d. analyzing the data.

D 19. Which of the following is a disadvantage of cross-sectional research?
a. It reveals little about the historical antecedents of behavior.
b. It provides no information about behavioral stability.
c. The results may be distorted by differences between cohorts.
d. All of the above.

B 20. To obtain a good picture of development within individuals, the investigator should employ
a. cross-sectional research.
b. longitudinal research.
c. vicarious reinforcement.
d. random selection.

A 21. Which of the following is *not* a drawback of interview techniques?
a. inability to study subjective phenomena
b. lack of standardization
c. reliance on language as a medium of communication
d. susceptibility to motivational factors

C 22. The focus of observational techniques is on
a. thought processes.
b. cause-and-effect relationships.
c. actual behavior.
d. none of the above.

D 23. In an experiment designed to determine the effect of group pressure on conformity, group pressure is the
a. experimental variable.
b. control variable.
c. dependent variable.
d. independent variable.

A 24. To ensure that every member of the population being studied has the same change of being chosen for the study, researchers apply the principle of
a. random sampling.
b. reliability.
c. validity.
d. all of the above.

D 25. Ethics are a particular concern in research with
a. children.
b. the retarded.
c. prisoners.
d. all of the above.

Matching

A. Functions of theories:

____1. Describes conditions of study.
____2. Sets boundaries.
____3. Suggests possible relationships.
____4. Brings together existing data.

a. generative
b. descriptive
c. delimiting
d. integrative

B. Components of the personality:

____1. Rational part of the personality.
____2. Seeks constant and immediate gratification.
____3. Conscience or moral system.

a. id
b. ego
c. superego

C. Stages of cognitive development:

____1. Ability to symbolize.
____2. Ability to think about how things change.
____3. Ability to think abstractly.
____4. Hands-on, trial-and-error stage.

a. sensorimotor
b. preoperational
c. concrete operations
d. formal operations

ANSWERS

True or False

1. F
2. F
3. F
4. T
5. T
6. F
7. T
8. T
9. F
10. F
11. T
12. F
13. T
14. T
15. F
16. T
17. F
18. F
19. T

20. T
21. T
22. F
23. F
24. T
25. F

Sentence Completion

1. change
2. social policy
3. environment
4. heredity, environment
5. theory
6. passive, active
7. psychoanalytic, cognitive, behavior
8. phallic
9. trust
10. cognitive
11. sensorimotor

12

12. formal operations
13. input, output
14. recognition
15. verbal rehearsal, clustering (categorizing)
16. Ivan Pavlov
17. Skinner box
18. imitate (model)
19. broad, general
20. variables
21. cohort
22. observational
23. independent, dependent
24. standardized test
25. random selection

Matching

A. 1. b
   2. c
   3. a
   4. d

B. 1. b
   2. a
   3. c

C. 1. b
   2. c
   3. d
   4. a

Multiple Choice

1. c
2. b
3. c
4. d
5. a
6. c
7. d
8. a
9. b
10. a
11. b
12. d
13. c
14. a
15. b
16. d
17. c
18. b
19. d
20. b
21. a
22. c
23. d
24. a
25. d

Chapter 2

GENETICS, PREGNANCY, AND BIRTH

CHAPTER OUTLINE

The Process of Conception
    Alternative Methods of Conception
Genetic Foundations
    Mechanics of Heredity
    Genetic Transmission
        Dominant and Recessive Genes
        Sex Chromosomes
        Sex-Chromosome Abnormalities
    Influence of Genetics on Behavior
        Unraveling the Genetic Thread
        Physical Appearance and Disorders
        Personality
        Intelligence
    Genetic Counseling
Prenatal Development
    Stages
    Effects of the Prenatal Environment
        Maternal Conditions
        Mother's Emotional State
        Rh-Factor Incompatibility
        Teratogens
        A Note of Reassurance
Birth
    The Birth Process
    Complications
        Low-Birthweight Infants
        Childbirth Methods

SUMMARY OF KEY CONCEPTS

1.   *Conception* is the process by which the egg and sperm unite to form the *zygote*. The new cell grows by a process known as *mitosis*.

2.   Alternative methods of conception involve the use of a donated egg and sperm. They include *artificial insemination*, *in vitro fertilization*, and employing a *surrogate mother*.

3.   The growth and development of the fertilized egg are guided by its unique genetic programming. The *genes,* which are made up of molecules of DNA, are arranged on the *chromosomes* that are present in the nucleus of every living cell.

14

4. The *sex chromosomes* determine gender and sex-linked characteristics. Other chromosomes and genes determine physical features such as eye and skin color, height, and body proportions. Certain diseases are inherited via the genes, and studies of personality and intelligence suggest a genetic influence on these characteristics.

5. Prenatal diagnosis using *amniocentesis* is one aspect of genetic counseling, in which parents can obtain information about the possible characteristics of their offspring.

PRE-NATAL GROWTH

3 STAGES

6. Prenatal development involves three stages of growth. In the *ovum stage*, the zygote enters the uterus and becomes embedded in the uterine wall. In the *embryo stage*, the cells differentiate into different systems and organs. In the *fetal stage*, the fetus increases in size until birth occurs.

1. OUUM
2. EMBRYO
3. FETAL

7. The prenatal period is a critical period in development, during which the unborn child is vulnerable to unborn influences. The physical condition of the mother is one such influence. Others include *teratogens*--specific environmental agents such as drugs, bacteria, and radiation.

BIRTH PROCESS —
3 STAGES:

8. The birth process has three stages: dilation of the cervix, delivery of the baby, and delivery of the placenta and umbilical cord.

1. DILATION OF CERVIX
2. DELIVERY OF BABY.

9. Complications of the birth process include *breech birth, Caesarian section, anoxia,* and low birthweight. Drugs used in labor and delivery affect the alertness of the newborn.

3. DELIVERY OF PLACENTA

10. Prepared-childbirth classes and new methods of delivery can help parents be more relaxed during birth and better prepared to establish contact with their newborn infant.

KEY TERMS AND PHRASES

germ cells — THE EGG OR SPERM CELL
fertilization — EGG & SPERM UNITE.
zygote — COMBO OF EGG & SPERM
mitosis — ZYGOTE GROWTH
infertility — INABILITY OR DIFFICULTY IN CONCEIVING
artificial insemination
chromosomes — ROD LIKE STRUCTURES CONTAINING GENES
genes — SEGMENTS OF DNA
deoxyribonucleic acid — DNA — PROTEIN MOLECULE
meiosis — PROCESS OF CELL DIVISION
monozygotic twins — TWINS FORMED FROM ONE EGG
dizygotic twins —   "   "   "   TWO EGGS
alleles — SINGLE GENES "
dominance
recessiveness
dominant gene

15

recessive gene
sex chromosome
autosomes — 22 PAIR OF CHROMOSOMES
prenatal diagnosis
amniocentesis
ovum stage
differentiation — CHANGES IN GROWTH & DEVELOPMENT
blastocyst — HOLLOW SPHERE OF CELLS THAT FORMS WITHIN A WEEK OF FERTILIZA
embryo stage — FIRST SIX WEEKS AFTER FERTILIZATION
placenta — BLOOD FILLED STRUCTURE THAT NOURISHES UNBORN CHILD
umbilical cord — LINKS EMBRYO TO PLACENTA
ectoderm
mesoderm
endoderm
critical period
fetal stage
quickening
teratogens — SPECIFIC ENVIRONMENTAL AGENTS AFFECTING FETUS
(DRUGS, BACTERIA, RADIATION)
labor
cervix — OPENING TO UTERUS
crowning
breech birth
Caesarian section
anoxia — LACK OF OXYGEN TO BABY @ BIRTH
short-gestation-period babies
small-for-date babies
prepared childbirth
Lamaze method
birthing rooms

REVIEW QUESTIONS

1. What alternatives to normal means of conception are available? What are some issues related to the use of those alternatives?

① ARTIFICIAL INSEMINATION   ② IN VITRO FERTILIZATION
③ SURROGATE MOTHER

2. Briefly describe the mechanics of heredity.

CHROMOSOMES CONTAIN GENES; GENES ARE SEGMENTS OF DNA; DNA CARRIES "INSTRUCTIONS"

3. What is meant by dominant and recessive genes?

4. How does a person's genetic heritage influence his or her appearance, personality, and intelligence?

5. What are the stages of prenatal development?

OVUM, EMBRYO, FETUS

6. In what ways does the prenatal environment affect the unborn child?

7. Briefly describe the birth process and some complications that may occur during that process.

EXERCISES

1. Describe the three main stages of prenatal development:

STAGE	TIME PERIOD	DESCRIPTION
Ovum Stage		
Embryo Stage		
Fetal Stage		

2. Note the effects of the following teratogens on the developing fetus:

TERATOGEN	EFFECTS
Prescribed and over-the-counter drugs	
Antibiotics	
Heroin, morphine	
Alcohol	

Maternal smoking

_____

Caffeine

_____

Rubella (German
measles)

_____

Toxoplasmosis

_____

Untreated maternal
syphilis

_____

Hormones

_____

Radiation and envir-
onmental hazards

_____

QUIZ

<u>True or False</u>

F 1. In a healthy mature female, a ripened egg is released from one ovary every twenty-one days.

F 2. Although "test-tube babies" are a frequent theme in science fiction, no human infant has ever been conceived in a test tube.

T 3. As a result of advances in alternative methods of conception, it is now possible for a child to have five parents.

T 4. The chromosomes are located in the nucleus of each cell in the human body.

F 5. Each chromosome holds 46 pairs of genes.

T 6. Monozygotic twins are formed when the zygote divides into two separate cells during mitosis.

18

F___7. Disorders such as phenylketonuria, hemophilia, and sickle-cell anemia are carried on recessive genes.

F___8. Recent research has shown that almost all human behavior can be traced to genetic factors.

T___9. Comparisons of monozygotic and dizygotic twins are especially important in distinguishing the effects of training and environment from those of heredity.

F___10. Genetic differences have been shown to explain about 75 percent of the variance in IQ scores.

F___11. Amniocentesis is a procedure that is used to terminate a pregnancy when the infant is likely to be deformed.

T___12. A normal pregnancy lasts 266 days.

F___13. During the embryo stage of prenatal development, the developing ovum travels to the uterus and becomes implanted in the uterine wall.

T___14. The skin, sense organs, and nervous system develop from the ectoderm.

F___15. The term *quickening* refers to the fetus's startle response to loud extrauterine noises.

F___16. The placental barrier prevents nonbeneficial substances from reaching the embryo or fetus.

T___17. Down syndrome can be caused by a faulty sperm fertilizing a healthy egg.

T___18. Inadequate maternal nutrition poses the greatest potential threat to the development of the unborn child.

F___19. The mother's emotional state has no effect on the intrauterine environment.

T___20. The developing child is most vulnerable to teratogens during the first trimester of pregnancy.

F___21. There is no scientific evidence for a connection between alcohol consumption during pregnancy and faulty development of the fetus.

F___22. There is a strong link between viral diseases and birth defects.

T___23. Ninety-five percent of all live births are healthy and well formed.

F___24. The Apgar scale is used to assess the infant's intelligence at birth.

T___25. Anoxia, or lack of oxygen immediately after birth, can cause severe brain damage.

Sentence Completion

1. Fertilization of the egg by the sperm usually occurs in the _FALLOPIAN TUBE_.

2. _IN ULTRO_ fertilization occurs in a test tube.

3. A woman who is hired to become pregnant by artificial insemination is known as a _SUR_.

4. Within the nucleus of every human cell are rodlike structures called _CHROMOSOMES_, each of which is made up of long segments called _GENES_.

5. The egg and sperm are referred to as _GERM_ cells.

6. Fraternal or _DIZYGOTIC_ twins are formed when the mother's body releases two egg cells that are fertilized by different sperm cells.

7. The genetic arrangement contained in the cells of an individual is his or her _GENOTYPE_

8. Of the 46 chromosomes within each human cell, 22 pairs are referred to as _AUTOSOMES_

9. _GENETICS_ is the study of the effects of heredity on behavior.

10. Down syndrome is more frequently found in offspring of _OLDER_ mothers.

11. Infant _TEMPERAMENT_ (e.g., irritability and sociability) has been found to be strongly influenced by genetics.

12. Overall, research has found a closer relationship in intelligence between adopted children and their _BIOLOGICAL_ parents than between those children and their _ADOPTIVE_ parents.

13. A process known as _AMNIOCENTESIS_ can be used to determine the chromosomal, genetic, and metabolic characteristics of an unborn child.

14. The first stage of prenatal development is the _OVUM_ stage.

15. The _AMNIOTIC SAC_ is a membrane filled with a salty solution that surrounds the embryo.

16. The layer of the embryo from which the circulatory, excretory, and musculatory systems develop is the _MESODERM_

17. By the _7th_ month of pregnancy the fetus has a chance of surviving outside the uterus if born prematurely.

18. Severe maternal malnutrition can have a profound effect on the development of the baby's _NERVOUS_ system.

20

19. When the blood of an Rh+ person is mixed with the blood of an Rh- person, the Rh- person's body reacts by producing _ANTIBODIES_

20. The scientific study of defects in newborns caused by the influence of the prenatal environment is called _TERATOLOGY_

21. Women who smoke heavily are twice as likely to deliver _low-BIRTHWEIGHT_ babies as nonsmoking mothers.

22. _TOXOPLASMOSIS_ is a parasitic infection that can result in damage to the eyes, ears, and brain of the fetus.

23. During the first stage of labor the _CERVIX_ is dilated by the action of uterine contractions.

24. In a _BREECH_, the baby appears at the vagina in a bottom-first position.

25. In _PREPARED CHILDBIRTH_ classes prospective parents learn about the stages of labor, hospital obstetric routines, and specific exercises to use during labor.

Multiple Choice

_C_ 1. The new cell that results from fertilization is known as a (an)
   a. germ cell.
   b. autosome.
   c. zygote.
   d. egg cell.

_B_ 2. A procedure in which fertilization occurs outside the uterus is known as
   a. artificial insemination.
   b. in vitro fertilization.
   c. surrogacy.
   d. none of the above; such a procedure is not possible.

_A_ 3. Throughout development, the physical changes that occur in the body are directed by the
   a. genes.
   b. phenotype.
   c. teratogens.
   d. germ cells.

_B_ 4. Fraternal twins are
   a. monozygotic.
   b. dizygotic.
   c. unizygotic.
   d. multizygotic.

_C_ 5. To inherit a trait that is carried on a recessive gene, a person must receive
   a. a dominant gene from both parents.
   b. a dominant gene from one parent and a recessive gene from the other parent.
   c. a recessive gene from both parents.
   d. any of the above.

_D_ 6. Hemophilia is an example of a
   a. sex-chromosome abnormality.
   b. teratogenic disorder.
   c. complication of childbirth.
   d. sex-linked recessive disorder.

_D_ 7. Studies of the impact of genetics on human behavior are usually conducted by means of
   a. selective breeding.
   b. construction of family trees.
   c. cell biopsies.
   d. comparison of twin pairs.

_C_ 8. Which of the following statements is *not* true?
   a. Heredity has a strong influence on physical appearance.
   b. Environmental factors can alter the effects of genetic factors.
   c. The genetic influence on physical development ceases when the individual reaches adulthood.
   d. Researchers can agree on a description of an individual's phenotype for physical appearance.

_A_ 9. An infant's level of activity, sleep patterns, irritability, and sociability are referred to as its
   a. temperament.
   b. genotype.
   c. intelligence quotient.
   d. none of the above.

_B_ 10. According to recent data, genetic differences appear to explain what proportion of the variance in IQ scores?
   a. 25 percent
   b. 50 percent
   c. 75 percent
   d. 100 percent

_A_ 11. Genetic defects in a fetus can be identified by means of
   a. amniocentesis.
   b. ultrasound.
   c. prenatal surgery.
   d. the Lamaze method.

_A_ 12. During which stage of prenatal development does the process of differentiation begin?
   a. the ovum stage
   b. the embryo stage
   c. the fetal stage
   d. the critical period

_C_ 13. The digestive, respiratory, and glandular systems emerge from the
   a. ectoderm.
   b. mesoderm.
   c. endoderm.
   d. gonadal tissue.

_D_ 14. During which stage of development does the fetus grow most rapidly?
   a. the first six weeks
   b. the second trimester
   c. the seventh month
   d. the last two months

_B_ 15. In the early 1960s the birth of grossly deformed babies was linked to the drug
   a. diethylstilbestrol.
   b. Thalidomide.
   c. teratogen.
   d. hexachlorophene.

_D_ 16. Mothers over 35 are more likely to
   a. have stillborn babies.
   b. give birth to a child with Down syndrome.
   c. have long, difficult labors.
   d. all of the above.

_A_ 17. Severe maternal malnutrition results in babies with
   a. low levels of intellectual functioning.
   b. physical deformities.
   c. growth deficiencies.
   d. toxoplasmosis.

_C_ 18. Which of the following statements is *not* true?
   a. The Rh factor is an inherited, genetically dominant trait.
   b. When blood from an Rh+ fetus mixes with that of an Rh- mother, the mother's body produces Rh antibodies.
   c. Rh incompatibility results in a stillborn infant.
   d. Rh disease can be predicted and prevented through genetic counseling.

_B_ 19. Growth deficiencies, facial malformations, and central nervous system dysfunctions are among the symptoms of
   a.   Rh disease.
   b.   fetal alcohol syndrome.
   c.   toxoplasmosis.
   d.   fetal syphilis.

_A_ 20. A maternal disease that can cause blindness, deafness, and other defects in an unborn child is
   a.   rubella.
   b.   influenza.
   c.   chicken pox.
   d.   infectious hepatitis.

_D_ 21. Excessive exposure to radiation can cause
   a.   stillbirths.
   b.   miscarriages.
   c.   gross deformities.
   d.   all of the above.

_C_ 22. The first stage of labor ends with dilation of the
   a.   vaginal opening.
   b.   uterus.
   c.   cervix.
   d.   birth canal.

_A_ 23. On the Apgar scale, the presence of a life-threatening condition is indicated by a score of
   a.   0.
   b.   1.
   c.   2.
   d.   10.

_B_ 24. The procedure in which a newborn is extracted from the uterus through an incision in the abdominal wall is termed
   a.   amniocentesis.
   b.   Caesarian section.
   c.   episiotomy.
   d.   surrogacy.

_D_ 25. The Lamaze method is a form of
   a.   prenatal diagnosis.
   b.   artificial insemination.
   c.   fetal surgery.
   d.   prepared childbirth.

Matching

A. Stages of prenatal development:

_A_ _E_ 1. Ovum stage
_D_ _F_ 2. Embryo stage
_B_ _C_ 3. Fetal stage

   a. Lasts approximately 2 weeks.
   b. Completion of body structures.
   c. First real bone cells appear.
   d. From Greek word meaning "to swell."
   e. Also called the germinal stage.
   f. Considered the most vulnerable and sensitive stage.

B. Layers of the embryo:

_C_ 1. Ectoderm

_A_ 2. Mesoderm

_B_ 3. Endoderm

   a. Middle layer, from which the circulatory, excretory, and muscular systems develop.
   b. Inner layer, from which the respiratory and glandular systems emerge.
   c. Outer layer, from which the skin, sense organs, and nervous system develop.

C. Stages of the birth process:

_B_ 1. Stage 1
_A_ 2. Stage 2
_C_ 3. Stage 3

   a. Crowning occurs.
   b. Cervix is dilated.
   c. Placenta is delivered.

ANSWERS

True or False

1. F
2. F
3. T
4. T
5. F
6. T
7. F
8. F
9. T
10. F
11. T
12. T
13. F
14. T
15. F
16. F
17. T
18. T
19. F
20. T
21. F
22. F
23. T
24. F
25. T

Sentence Completion

1. fallopian tube
2. in vitro
3. surrogate mother
4. chromosomes, genes
5. germ
6. dizygotic
7. genotype
8. autosomes
9. behavior genetics
10. older
11. temperament
12. biological, adoptive
13. amniocentesis
14. ovum
15. amniotic sac
16. mesoderm
17. seventh
18. nervous
19. antibodies
20. teratology
21. low-birthweight
22. toxoplasmosis
23. cervix
24. breech birth
25. prepared childbirth

21. d
22. c
23. a
24. b
25. d

Matching

A. 1. a, e
   2. d, f
   3. b, c

B. 1. c
   2. a
   3. b

C. 1. b
   2. a
   3. c

Multiple Choice

1. c
2. b
3. a.
4. b
5. c
6. d
7. d
8. c
9. a
10. b
11. a
12. a
13. c
14. d
15. b
16. d
17. a
18. c
19. b
20. a

Chapter 3

INFANCY: PHYSICAL, PERCEPTUAL, AND COGNITIVE DEVELOPMENT

CHAPTER OUTLINE

SUMMARY OF KEY CONCEPTS

1. The neonate's physiological systems must adjust to life outside the uterus. Respiration and circulation of oxygen begin when the umbilical cord is cut, but the digestive system may not function smoothly for several days.

2. Newborns experience six different states of consciousness: regular sleep, irregular sleep, drowsiness, alert inactivity, waking activity, and the crying state. It is most attentive to its environment when it is in the alert inactivity state.

3. Although the newborn's visual skills are limited, infants can see at birth and prefer to look at complex, symmetrical, high-contrast designs. The newborn's behavioral responses include *neonatal reflexes,* responses triggered by specific stimuli in the environment; these reflexes disappear as the nervous system matures.

4. Premature babies are not fully developed and require special environments if they are to survive. New medical technology is allowing more premature infants to survive than in the past.

5. Physical growth in infancy follows a *cephalocaudal* and *proximodistal* pattern. The infant develops more specific, controlled behaviors as the nervous system matures.

6. Motor development is guided by maturation and follows a predictable sequence. Prehension and locomotion are among the motor skills acquired during infancy.

7. Perception involves the interpretation of sensory information. Infants can recognize faces and perceive depth at an early age. Infants are able to recognize objects because they have encoded features of the objects into memory.

8. According to Piaget, during the *sensorimotor period* the infant acquires object permanence, learns to control its body and understand cause and effect, and begins to think in images.

9. According to learning theorists, cognitive development consists of a series of changes in learned behaviors. Behaviors are acquired through *classical* and *operant conditioning* and through *observational learning.*

KEY TERMS AND PHRASES

neonate - Infant during 1st weeks of life
lanugo - Fine hair covering newborns body
vernix caseosa - Cheese like covering "
molded (bones of skull) - during birth process
fontanelles - openings
apnea - Regular breathing stops
physiological neonatal jaundice -
colostrum early secretion from breast
rapid eye movement (REM) - phase of sleep
pupillary reflex iris
binocular fixation - focus both eyes
visual accommodation - ability to change shape of lens to focus
reflexes
neonatal reflexes - automatic responses
cephalocaudal - head to foot
proximodistal - inner to outer
myelin - protective sheath around neurons
cognition

assimilation
scheme
accommodation
object permanence
AB error — *Infant's ability to find object that's been put in a different place.*
classical conditioning
operant conditioning
reinforcement
positive reinforcement
negative reinforcement
punishment
observational learning

REVIEW QUESTIONS

1. Briefly describe the major physiological changes that occur during the first few weeks after birth.

2. What are the six states of consciousness experienced by newborns?

3. What reflexes are present in the newborn infant?

4. What factors contribute to the birth of premature and low-birthweight infants?

5. What is meant by the terms *cephalocaudal* and *proximodistal*?

6. What is sudden infant death syndrome? What causes it?

7. What are the two major motor skills that develop in infancy? What advances in perceptual ability are made in the first few months?

8. What is meant by assimilation and accommodation?

9. List the six substages of the sensorimotor period of cognitive growth as described in Piaget's theory.

10. Distinguish between classical and operant conditioning.

EXERCISES

1. Characteristics of the neonate/infant:

_____

Average weight at birth:

_____

Average length at birth:

_____

Skin characteristics:

_____

Eye color:

_____

Heart rate:

_____

Vision:

_____

Hearing:

_____

Smell:

_____

Taste:

_____

Reflexes:

_____

2. Substages of the sensorimotor period:

SUBSTAGE	APPROX. AGE	CHARACTERISTICS
1. Reflex		

_____

2. Primary
circular reactions

3. Secondary
circular reactions

4. Coordination of
secondary schemes

5. Tertiary
circular reactions

6. Invention of new
means through new
combinations

QUIZ

True or False

F 1. During the early weeks of life the infant is referred to as a zygote.

F 2. Most Caucasian infants have brown irises.

T 3. The colostrum secreted by the mother's breasts immediately after giving birth is a high-protein food source.

F 4. Infants are most attentive to their environment when they are in the crying state.

T 5. Habituation is a process in which a person becomes less sensitive to a stimulus.

T 6. Newborn babies are not capable of visual accommodation.

F 7. Researchers have found that infants respond more to continuous presentations of a sound than to complex patterns of sounds.

T 8. Neonatal reflexes are present only in the early weeks and months of life.

F 9. Preterm infants with birthweights below 1500 grams have no chance of survival.

31

F 10. Girls are more vulnerable than boys to delays in mental and motor development as a result of premature birth.

T 11. The term *cephalocaudal* refers to a head-to-foot pattern of physical and motor development.

F 12. At birth the brain is about 50 percent of adult weight.

T 13. Infants of young mothers are most susceptible to sudden infant death syndrome.

F 14. There is no significant difference between breast milk and cow's milk.

T 15. Most babies can begin feeding themselves by their first birthday.

T 16. The two major motor skills that develop in infancy are prehension and locomotion.

F 17. Recent research has shown that the infant's environment has no effect on its motor development.

T 18. Infants only 21 days old are able to imitate simple facial responses modeled by adults.

F 19. Infants cannot use the relative size of objects as a cue for distance until they are at least 7 months old.

T 20. The idea that knowledge is constructed is central to Piaget's theory of cognitive development.

F 21. According to Piaget, the first stage of cognitive development is the preoperational stage.

F 22. According to Piaget, curiosity is present in the infant from the age of about 6 months.

T 23. Between the ages of 8 and 12 months, infants begin to develop the concept of object permanence.

F 24. The term *symbolic thought* refers to the ability to respond to a signal such as the sound of a refrigerator door opening.

T 25. According to learning theorists, developmental changes in infants' reactions to their world occur exclusively as a result of the infant's experiences.

Sentence Completion

1. A neonate's body may be covered with fine hair called *lanugo*.

2. The rapid, shallow breathing of newborns may stop suddenly, a condition called
apnea

3. According to Peter Wolff, newborns experience __6__ separate stages of consciousness.

4. One way of studying infants' sensory capabilities is to measure their *physiological* reactions to sensory stimuli.

5. The automatic reaction of the iris to light is called the *pupillary reflex*

6. The ability to use both eyes simultaneously to focus on an object is termed
binocular fixation

7. Newborns have a preference for *sweet* tastes.

8. The *moro* reflex occurs when the infant is stimulated by a very loud noise.

9. The term *low birthweight* is used to describe infants who are born weighing less than *2500* grams.

10. The term *proximodistal* refers to physical and motor development in which the center of the body changes earlier and more rapidly than the extremities.

11. During infancy the bones harden, or *ossify*, at different rates.

12. *SIDS* is the name given to the sudden and unexpected death of seemingly healthy babies between the ages of 3 weeks and 1 year.

13. One advantage of breast feeding for the mother is that it stimulates the
uterus

14. During the first year of life the number of *fat* cells in a baby's body is determined by how much it eats.

15. The order of motor events is believed to be a result of *maturational* factors.

16. *Perception* involves the interpretation of sensory information.

17. An apparatus that is used to study infants' depth perception is known as the
visual cliff

18. *Cognition* is the process by which a person acquires and organizes information and knowledge about the world.

19. *Assimilation* is the process by which a person, using existing knowledge, takes in new information about the environment.

20. *Object permanence* is the knowledge that objects still exist even when they are not in sight.

21. The term *circular* refers to the infant's tendency to repeat activities that create a desirable action.

22. If an object is moved from one hiding place to another, a 1-year-old will continue to look in the original hiding place. The infant has developed *contextual* object permanence.

23. Infants in the *tertiary circular reaction* stage are curious and actively engaged in trying out new ways to accomplish their goals.

24. *Deferred imitation* is the ability to imitate an action in the absence of the model demonstrating that action.

25. *Operant conditioning* is a learning process in which the learner repeats behaviors that have resulted in a positive outcome and eliminates behaviors that have resulted in a negative outcome.

Multiple Choice

B 1. The cheesy substance coating the skin of a neonate is called
   a. lanugo.
   b. vernix caseosa.
   c. colostrum.
   d. SIDS.

D 2. The average newborn infant weighs
   a. less than 5 pounds.
   b. about 5 pounds.
   c. between 6 and 7 pounds.
   d. 7.5 pounds.

A 3. In the condition known as apnea, the infant's breathing
   a. stops suddenly.
   b. becomes rapid and shallow.
   c. becomes deep and irregular.
   d. is interrupted by coughs, sneezes, and wheezes.

C 4. Physiological neonatal jaundice occurs because
   a. the open spaces in the skull have not come together.
   b. the skin lacks a layer of insulating fat.
   c. the liver cannot break down bilirubin fast enough.
   d. the throat is filled with mucus, making it difficult for the infant to suck.

C 5. What portion of the infant's sleep is spent in REM sleep?
   a. none
   b. 25 percent
   c. 50 percent
   d. almost all

34

_B_ 6. The process by which a person becomes familiar with a stimulus and also less sensitive to it is known as
a. preferential looking.
b. habituation.
c. visual accommodation.
d. the Moro reflex.

_D_ 7. The ability to use both eyes simultaneously to focus on an object is known as
a. visual accommodation.
b. visual acuity.
c. the pupillary reflex.
d. binocular fixation.

_A_ 8. Newborns prefer to look at visual patterns that are
a. symmetrical.
b. nonconcentric.
c. relatively low in contrast.
d. based on straight lines.

_D_ 9. Newborns are able to
a. distinguish between high- and low-pitched tones.
b. distinguish between loud and soft sounds.
c. locate a sound in space.
d. all of the above.

_C_ 10. Which of the following reflexes disappears in the first few months of life?
a. the pupillary reflex
b. gagging
c. the sucking reflex
d. none of the above

_A_ 11. The Moro reflex occurs when
a. the infant is stimulated by a very loud noise.
b. the baby's cheek is stroked.
c. the sole of the foot is stimulated.
d. an object is placed in the palm of the newborn's hand.

_B_ 12. Which of the following statements is *not* true?
a. Preterm infants are more vulnerable to complications and delays in development than full-term infants.
b. Preterm infants sleep less than full-term infants.
c. The younger and smaller the infant at birth, the more problems there are in later development.
d. Differences between full-term and preterm infants diminish with age.

_B_ 13. The term *proximodistal* is used to refer to a pattern of development in which
   a. development occurs first and more rapidly in the head and upper parts of the body.
   b. development occurs early and more rapidly in the center of the body.
   c. general, less specific reactions are replaced by more controlled, specific reactions.
   d. neonatal reflexes are replaced by learned behaviors.

_D_ 14. Sudden infant death syndrome occurs most frequently in babies
   a. who were born prematurely.
   b. whose mothers are young.
   c. whose mothers smoke.
   d. all of the above.

_C_ 15. Which of the following statements is *not* true?
   a. Breast milk is more readily digested by the infant than cow's milk.
   b. Breast feeding stimulates the mother's uterus.
   c. The quantity of milk produced by the mother increases rapidly in the first 2 weeks and remains constant thereafter.
   d. Most babies begin drinking from a cup when they are 6 to 8 months old.

_A_ 16. The two major motor skills that develop in infancy are
   a. prehension and locomotion.
   b. palmar grasp and pincer grasp.
   c. creeping and walking.
   d. eye-hand coordination and unassisted walking.

_B_ 17. Perception refers to
   a. gathering information via the senses.
   b. interpreting sensory information.
   c. imitating the facial responses of adults.
   d. touching and manipulating objects.

_B_ 18. The "visual cliff" is used to determine whether the infant can
   a. distinguish between a happy face and a fearful one.
   b. perceive that an object has depth or solidity.
   c. tell how far away an object is.
   d. acquire and organize information about the world.

_D_ 19. Young infants are able to
   a. attend.
   b. select.
   c. remember.
   d. all of the above.

_C_ 20. Piaget used the term *schemes* to refer to
    a.   neonatal reflexes.
    b.   conditioned responses.
    c.   action sequences.
    d.   behaviors modeled by adults.

_C_ 21. Which of the following is *not* a cognitive task that the infant has accomplished by the age of 2?
    a.   The recognition that events are preceded by some cause.
    b.   The knowledge that objects still exist even when not in sight.
    c.   The ability to think about how things change.
    d.   The ability to use symbols in language and thought.

_A_ 22. The stage in which the infant's actions are focused more on objects and events outside its own body is the stage of
    a.   secondary circular reactions.
    b.   primary circular reactions.
    c.   coordination of secondary schemes.
    d.   coordination of tertiary schemes.

_D_ 23. A child that will search for a toy that has been secretly hidden has mastered the concept of
    a.   deferred imitation.
    b.   signal meaning.
    c.   cognition.
    d.   object permanence.

_A_ 24. The process in which a neutral stimulus is paired with a stimulus that automatically elicits a particular response until the neutral stimulus alone will elicit that response is known as
    a.   classical conditioning.
    b.   operant conditioning.
    c.   positive reinforcement.
    d.   negative reinforcement.

_C_ 25. In which of the following processes does the child imitate the specific behaviors of a model?
    a.   classical conditioning
    b.   operant conditioning
    c.   observational learning
    d.   reinforced practice

Matching

A. States of infant consciousness:

_C_ 1. Drowsiness

_D_ 2. Alert inactivity

_F_ 3. Crying state

_A_ 4. Regular sleep

_B_ 5. Irregular sleep

_E_ 6. Waking activity

a. Infant breathes smoothly and evenly; eyes are closed.
b. Infant's breathing is uneven; REM occurs.
c. Infant's eyes open and close intermittently.
d. Infant is awake with relaxed face.
e. Infant is awake and occasionally displays motor movement.
f. Infant has facial grimace and displays motor movement.

B. Reflexes present in the infant:

_D_ 1. Palmar grasp

_G_ 2. Babinski

_F_ 3. Stepping

_B_ 4. Sucking

_A_ 5. Moro

_E_ 6. Rooting

_C_ 7. Babkin

a. Reflex elicited when the baby is stimulated by a loud noise or sudden removal of support.
b. The baby sucks rhythmically when a nipple or finger is placed in its mouth.
c. Mouth opens, eyes close, and head turns to side when baby's palms are pressed.
d. Fingers flex and enclose object when palm is touched.
e. When cheek is stroked, head turns in the direction of the stimulus.
f. Rhythmic walking movements when baby is held in upright position.
g. Toes fan out when heel is stroked.

C. Substages of sensorimotor development:

_D_ 1. Reflex

_F_ 2. Primary circular

_A_ 3. Secondary circular reactions

_B_ 4. Coordination of secondary reactions

_E_ 5. Tertiary circular reactions

_C_ 6. Invention of new means through mental combinations

a. Modifications are made in the object permanence scheme.
b. Infant uses accumulated knowledge to produce an effect.
c. Infant can form a mental picture.
d. Infant "exercises" ready-made sensorimotor schemes.
e. New schemes are created through active exploration and experimentation.
f. Infant repeats activity that creates desirable action.

ANSWERS

1. F
2. F
3. T
4. F
5. T
6. T
7. F
8. T
9. F
10. F
11. T
12. F
13. T
14. F
15. T
16. T
17. F
18. T
19. F
20. T
21. F
22. F
23. T
24. F
25. T

Sentence Completion

1. lanugo
2. apnea
3. six
4. physiological
5. pupillary reflex
6. binocular fixation
7. sweet
8. Moro
9. 2500
10. proximodistal
11. ossify
12. sudden infant death syndrome
13. uterus
14. fat
15. maturational
16. perception
17. visual cliff
18. cognition
19. assimilation
20. object permanence
21. circular
22. contextually bound
23. tertiary circular reaction
24. deferred imitation
25. operant conditioning

Multiple Choice

1. b
2. d
3. a
4. c
5. c
6. b
7. d
8. a
9. d
10. c
11. a
12. b
13. b
14. d
15. c
16. a
17. b
18. b
19. d
20. c
21. c
22. a
23. d
24. a
25. c

Matching

A. 1. c
   2. d
   3. f
   4. a
   5. b
   6. e

B. 1. d
   2. g
   3. f
   4. b
   5. a
   6. e
   7. c

C. 1. d
   2. f
   3. a
   4. b
   5. e
   6. c

Chapter 4

INFANCY:
SOCIAL AND PERSONALITY DEVELOPMENT

CHAPTER OUTLINE

SUMMARY OF KEY CONCEPTS

1. The infant's earliest social interactions are with parents. In the *bidirectional view* of development, the parent and child are seen as having an active influence on each other.

2. An infant's physical appearance, health, and maturity may influence a parent's initial reactions to the infant. Differences in infant temperaments also elicit differing reactions from caregivers.

3. Infants are capable of expressing a progressively greater variety of emotions during the first two years of life. One way to assess infant emotions is to rate changes in facial expression in response to different emotional experiences.

4. The early interactions between parent and child form the basis of Erikson's first developmental stage: basic trust versus mistrust. A consistent and affectionate caregiver helps the child negotiate this stage successfully.

5. Research on parent-child interactions suggests that parents who stimulate, touch, and hold their infants and express warm, positive emotions toward them are likely to have more responsive and socially competent infants. Social support given to parents in times of stress is also likely to foster a positive parent-child relationship.

6. The *attachment* between parent and child begins at birth and is clearly established by the age of six to twelve months. Attachment is indicated by the child's seeking contact with the caregiver, by the degree of distress shown by the child upon separation from the caregiver or when a stranger is present, and by the extent to which a child can use the caregiver to recover from stress.

7. Children may have more than one attachment figure and often become attached to the father as well as the mother. Fathers and mothers tend to interact with their infants in different ways.

8. Three patterns of attachment have been observed: secure, insecure-resistant, and insecure-avoidant. Most children are securely attached.

9. The toddler begins to separate from the parent and to develop a sense of autonomy. If demands on the child for self-control are too rigid, the child may develop feelings of shame and self-doubt. The sense of self begins in late infancy and continues to develop throughout childhood.

10. Prelanguage behavior occurs in infancy in the form of crying, cooing, and gesturing. Mothers have a particular way of talking to their babies to main social contact with them.

KEY TERMS AND PHRASES

unidirectional view — Child seen as passive, recipient
bidirectional view — " & parent - active influences on ea other
temperament
attachment

REVIEW QUESTIONS

1. What is meant by the bidirectional view of development?

2. List the nine characteristics of infant temperament.

3. Briefly describe the emotions observed in infants. How are infant emotions assessed?

4. What is the crisis that must be resolved in Erikson's first stage of psychosocial development?

5. What is meant by attachment? How does it develop?

6. What are the three basic patterns of attachment?

7. How does self-awareness develop in the infant?

8. Briefly describe the stages of language development in the first two years.

9. What is motherese?

EXERCISES

1. Use an X to indicate whether each of the following temperamental qualities describes an easy baby, a difficult baby, or a slow-to-warm baby.

BEHAVIOR	EASY	DIFFICULT	SLOW-TO-WARM
Adaptability			
Slow to adapt			
Readily adapts			
Reaction Intensity			
High			
Low			
Irritability Level			
High			
Low			

Eating/Sleeping
  Patterns
  Regular
  Irregular

Approachability
  Approachable
  Withdrawn

2. Briefly describe each phase in the development of attachment.

PHASE	AGE	DESCRIPTION
Preattachment		
Attachment-in-the-Making		
Clear-cut Attachment		
Goal-Corrected Partnership		

QUIZ

True or False

___F___1. All infants exhibit the same patterns of interaction with parents and other caregivers.

___F___2. Research since the late 1950s has shown that the interaction between parent and child is unidirectional.

___T___3. The newborn infant and its parents are primed to form a powerful affectional bond.

___F___4. Researchers generally agree that early and sustained physical contact between parent and child is necessary for the formation of an affectional bond.

44

_F_ 5. Mothers tend to pay less attention to preterm infants than to full-term infants.

_T_ 6. Infants have been found to differ in terms of nine qualities of behavior and reaction.

_T_ 7. "Difficult" babies have irregular patterns of eating and sleeping and adapt slowly to changes.

_T_ 8. The temperamental qualities of a newborn can be used to predict its emotional reactions later in infancy.

_F_ 9. Most infants do not exhibit social smiles before the age of three months.

_T_ 10. Infants' emotions are usually inferred from their facial expressions.

_F_ 11. Children begin to imitate adults' facial expressions at about 18 months of age. *earlier*

_T_ 12. According to Freud, personality develops during the oral stage of psychosexual development.

_F_ 13. According to Erikson, the first psychosocial crisis encountered by the child is the identity crisis.

_F_ 14. Mothers who are depressed are likely to interact with their infants in a highly responsive manner.

_T_ 15. Social support from family members and the community results in more positive relations between parents and their infants.

_F_ 16. John Bowlby was one of the earliest writers to call attention to the importance of infant temperament.

_T_ 17. Attachment refers to an organized system of parental and child behaviors that have an emotional quality.

_F_ 18. Stranger anxiety refers to the distress exhibited by an infant when its parents leave the room.

_T_ 19. Fathers tend to take more interest in their infant sons than in their daughters.

_T_ 20. The "strange situation" procedure is used to study patterns of attachment.

_F_ 21. The development of attachment follows the same pattern in institutionalized children as in noninstitutionalized children.

_T_ 22. Compared to insecurely attached children, securely attached children get along better with peers and preschool teachers.

_T_ 23. Foster parents are sometimes urged not to establish a close emotional bond with the child.

E_24. According to Erikson, the major task facing children between 1 1/2 and 3 years of age is to develop trust in other people.

T_25. According to Mahler, newborns are largely oblivious to events and people around them.

Sentence Completion

1. Until the late 1950s, the dominant view of infant development was _____.

2. Many parents will readily acknowledge that infants are capable of engaging in a _____, _____ social exchange.

3. Studies have shown that newborns in the first hours of life engage in behaviors that _____ the parent's actions.

4. Special attention may be needed for the parents of _____ newborns to promote a healthy parent-infant bond.

5. On the basis of temperamental qualities, babies can be classified into three categories: _____, _____, and _____.

6. Difficult behavior on the baby's part is _____ of a problem when they expected such behavior to emerge.

7. The infant begins to show positive and negative emotion at about _____ months.

8. In the first month the infant's smile is referred to as _____.

9. Specific facial expressions of _____ can be reliably detected in 7-month-old infants.

10. According to Freud, personality begins to develop when the young infant's _____ needs are met.

11. Parents who stimulate their infants generally have more _____ and _____ children.

12. Mothers who are depressed are likely to interact with their infants in an _____ and _____ manner.

13. A large number of child-abuse victims are _____ births.

14. Virtually all infants form an _____ to their caregiver.

15. Harry Harlow's experiments demonstrated that _____-raised monkeys were unable to establish healthy social behaviors.

16. John Bowlby identified _____ phases during which the infant gradually directs more of its attention toward being physically close to the caregiver.

17. According to Bowlby, in the _____ phase the attachment between the infant and the caregiver is characterized by a complex interplay of cognitive, social, and emotional behavior.

18. Observational studies of parents' interactions with infants have found that mothers more often engage in _____ while fathers more often engage in _____.

19. The procedure developed by Ainsworth and her associates to study patterns of attachment is known as the _____.

20. Individual differences in attachment patterns have been linked to the _____ of the caregiver-child interaction.

21. Insecurely attached children have been found to _____ their preschool peers.

22. Recent legislation in the United States has been directed at _____ the number and duration of foster care placements.

23. During the _____ stage of psychosexual development children learn how to delay gratification of their sensual needs.

24. In the _____ stage of individuation infants are preoccupied with their own internal sensations.

25. One way of measuring self-awareness is to assess the child's use of _____ words.

Multiple Choice

1. Until the late 1950s, most studies of infant behavior focused primarily on the effects of
   a.   differences in infant temperament.
   b.   different child-rearing practices.
   c.   the actions of the infant.
   d.   none of the above.

2. The view of development in which the parent and child are seen as influencing each other is the
   a.   unidirectional model.
   b.   monodirectional view.
   c.   multidirectional model.
   d.   bidirectional view.

_B_ 3. According to Klaus and Kennell, a powerful affectional bond between an infant and its parents is formed
   a. at the moment of birth.
   b. during the first few hours after birth.
   c. during the first few weeks after birth.
   d. at any point in the child's life; timing is irrelevant.

_A_ 4. According to Brazelton, a nurturant response on the part of adults is elicited by
   a. the shape of the infant.
   b. the norms of society.
   c. the hospital setting.
   d. none of the above; adults automatically nurture babies.

_C_ 5. Temperament is believed to be the first manifestation of the child's later
   a. intelligence
   b. autonomy vs. shame and doubt
   c. the oral stage
   d. the anal stage

_A_ 6. The largest percentage of newborns may be characterized as
   a. "easy."
   b. "difficult."
   c. "slow-to-warm."
   d. none of the above.

 7. Which of the following statements is *not* true?
   a. Measurements of an infant's temperament can be used to predict the strength of the infant's emotional reactions at 9 months.
   b. Parents are significantly influenced by whether an infant is easy, difficult, or slow-to-warm.
   c. Observers other than the parents are unable to assess an infant's temperament.
   d. Children who were active as neonates are more likely to be active at age 4.

 8. According to Sroufe, the infant begins to show an interest in the outside world in which stage of emotional development?
   a. stage 1
   b. stage 2
   c. stage 5
   d. stage 7

_D_ 9. According to Sroufe, which emotions emerge in the eighth stage of emotional development (around age 3)?
   a. anticipation and disappointment
   b. attachment and ambivalence
   c. joy and anger
   d. pride and guilt

_A_ 10. Infant emotions are commonly inferred from the baby's
    a. facial expressions.
    b. vocalizations.
    d. body language.
    d. temperament.

_D_ 11. Specific facial expressions of anger can be reliably detected in infants at the age of
    a. 18 months.
    b. 15 months.
    c. 10 months.
    d. 7 months.

_C_ 12. Which of the following is the first stage of psychosexual development?
    a. trust vs. mistrust
    b. autonomy vs. shame and doubt
    c. the oral stage
    d. the anal stage

_B_ 13. Which of the following statements is true?
    a. The development of trust is not related to the extent to which the infant's physical needs are met.
    b. A certain amount of frustration can help infants develop greater trust in themselves.
    c. Mistrustful infants develop a strong sense of themselves as worthy of attention.
    d. Parental characteristics do not affect the child's acquisition of basic trust in others.

_A_ 14. Which of the following statements is _not true?_
    a. Parents who stimulate their infants generally have more irritable babies.
    b. Insensitivity is the greatest obstacle to a child's development.
    c. Mothers who are depressed are likely to interact with their infants in an inconsistent manner.
    d. Young children are affected by angry exchanges even if the anger is not directed at them.

_C_ 15. The most helpful types of social support come from
    a. government agencies.
    b. medical personnel.
    c. friends and relatives.
    d. the preschool.

_D_ 16. The affectionate emotional bond between parents and their children is referred to by psychologists as
    a. motherese.
    b. symbiosis.
    c. goal-corrected partnership.
    d. attachment.

____17. In Bowlby's description of the development of attachment, the third phase is the
    a.   attachment-in-the-making phase.
    b.   preattachment phase.
    c.   goal-corrected partnership phase.
    d.   none of the above.

____18. Which of the following statements is *not* true?
    a.   Infants react positively to both mothers and fathers.
    b.   The quality of the father's involvement is an important determinant of the infant's reaction.
    c.   Fathers are less able than mothers to respond to infant cues that signal the need for care.
    d.   Fathers are more physical than mothers in their interaction with their infants.

____19. A procedure that is frequently used to study the attachment process is the
    a.   visual cliff.
    b.   strange situation.
    c.   Bowlby procedure.
    d.   terrycloth mother.

____20. An infant who uses the parent as a base for play and exploration is classified as
    a.   securely attached.
    b.   resistant, insecurely attached.
    c.   avoidant, insecurely attached.
    d.   none of the above.

____21. Which of the following statements is *not* true?
    a.   Researchers do not agree on the role of infant temperament in attachment patterns.
    b.   Differences in attachment have been linked to differences in the parents' behaviors.
    c.   The type of attachment an infant forms is influenced by the quality of the caregiver-child interaction.
    d.   None; they are all true.

____22. Recent legislation has been directed at reducing the extent of foster care because
    a.   most children in foster care would be better off with their parents.
    b.   foster parents tend to establish a close emotional bond with the child.
    c.   foster care tends to disrupt the infant's social and emotional development.
    d.   it is too expensive to train foster parents in correct child-rearing techniques.

_____23. According to Freud, during the anal stage of psychosexual development children learn to
    a.   trust other people.
    b.   delay gratification.
    c.   act autonomously.
    d.   use language.

_____24. In Mahler's theory of the development of self, the last phase is
    a.   separation individuation.
    b.   symbiosis.
    c.   the autistic phase.
    d.   none of the above.

_____25. Infant babbling emerges at
    a.   2 to 3 months.
    b.   4 to 5 months.
    c.   about 6 months.
    d.   about 9 months.

Matching

A. Periods of emotional development:

_C_ 1. Absolute stimulus barrier

_F_ 2. Turning toward

_A_ 3. Positive affect

H _B_ 4. Active participation

B _E_ 5. Attachment

C _E_ 6. Practicing

_G_ 7. Emergence of self

_D_ 8. Play and fantasy

a. Shows positive and negative emotions.
b. Shows strong positive feelings toward caregiver.
c. Shows no true emotions.
d. Evaluates performance using other people's standards.
e. Actively explores and masters environment.
f. Shows interest in outside world.
g. Experiences new-found sense of autonomy.
h. Makes efforts to elicit social responses from others.

B. Phases in the development of attachment:

____1. Preattachment
____2. Attachment-in-the-making
____3. Clear-cut attachment
____4. Goal-corrected partnership

a. The infant is likely to show signs of distress or protest when separated from its mother.
b. The infant is able to distinguish between the primary caregiver and others.
c. The infant may attempt to influence the attachment figure.
d. The infant does not distinguish among those with whom it comes into contact.

C. Phases of separation from the caregiver:

____1. Autistic phase
____2. Symbiosis
____3. Separation individuation

a. Infant and caregiver establish mutual dependency.
b. Infant recognizes itself as separate from caregiver.
c. Infant is preoccupied with its own internal sensations.

ANSWERS

<u>True or False</u>

1. F
2. F
3. T
4. F
5. F
6. T
7. T
8. T
9. F
10. T
11. F
12. T
13. F
14. F
15. T
16. F
17. T
18. F
19. T
20. T
21. F
22. T
23. T
24. F
25. T

<u>Sentence Completion</u>

1. unidirectional
2. dynamic, reciprocal
3. complement
4. ill
5. easy, difficult, slow-to-warm
6. less
7. three
8. endogenous
9. anger
10. oral
11. responsive, socially competent
12. inconsistent, nonresponsive
13. preterm
14. attachment
15. laboratory

16. four
17. goal-corrected partnership
18. routine child care, playful stimulation of the infant
19. strange situation
20. quality
21. avoid contact with
22. reducing
23. anal
24. autistic
25. self-referent

Multiple Choice

1. b
2. d
3. b
4. a
5. c
6. a
7. c
8. b
9. d
10. a
11. d
12. c
13. b
14. a
15. c
16. d
17. d
18. c
19. b
20. a
21. d
22. c
23. b
24. a
25. b

Matching

A. 1. c
    2. f
    3. a
    4. h
    5. b
    6. e
    7. g
    8. d

B. 1. d
    2. b
    3. a
    4. c

C. 1. c
    2. a
    3. b

Chapter 5

PRESCHOOL YEARS: PHYSICAL, COGNITIVE, AND LANGUAGE DEVELOPMENT

CHAPTER OUTLINE

1. Physical Development
 Size and Proportion
 Motor Coordination
  Gross Motor Coordination
  Fine Motor Coordination
2. Cognitive Development
 Piaget's Theory: The Preoperational Child
  Symbolic Function
  Symbolic Play and Imitation
  What Is Real
 Limitations of the Preoperational Thinker
  Egocentrism
  Concreteness
  Centration
  Irreversibility
  Transductive Reasoning
 Conceptual Understanding
  Time
  Number
  Classification
 Information Processing
  Attention
  Memory
3. Language Development
 Structure of Language
 Language Acquisition
  Semantic Development
  Syntactic Development
 Theories of Language Acquisition
 Bilingualism: Are Two Languages Better Than One?
4. Preschool and Day-Care Programs
 Types of Programs
  Nursery Schools
  Day Care
 Evaluating Preschool Programs
 Effects on Development
  Emotional Bonds
  Cognitive Skills
  Social Skills
 Conditions for Quality Day Care

SUMMARY OF KEY CONCEPTS

1. During the preschool years the rate of growth levels off as the shape and proportions of the child's body approximate those of an adult.

2. The gross motor skills become more coordinated, allowing the child to run, hop, skip, and jump. Fine motor skills take longer to develop, but by age 4 most children are able to handle tools and toys requiring such skills.

3. The symbolic function develops in the preoperational period. Preschool children can mentally represent their experience by means of language, gestures, deferred imitation, drawing, and symbolic play. They can also distinguish between physical reality and mental reality.

4. There are several limitations on preoperational thought: The child is egocentric, centers its attention on one perceptual attribute at a time, and is unable to use abstracts symbols. Also, the child cannot mentally reverse his or her thinking and engages in transductive reasoning.

5. Although most children can count by age 5, they have difficulty mastering conservation of number because they understand number in terms of perceptual cues such as density or length.

6. Preschool children attend to information in a haphazard manner and are easily distracted. They are less selective than older children about what they notice.

7. Young children's memory is limited by the fact that they do not classify items for memory storage and have not developed a way to rehearse and memorize groups of items.

8. Language development involves acquiring sounds or phonemes, learning the meanings of words, and acquiring the rules for combining words into sentences. Children begin to acquire language at age 2 and have mastered the essentials of their native language by age 6.

9. Preschool and day care are increasingly common experiences for young children. Research on day care indicates that it has no adverse effects on development, although infants' attachment to parents may be adversely affected.

KEY TERMS AND PHRASES

handedness – *PERSON'S BASIC PREFERENCE FOR USE OF ONE HAND OVER OTHER.*

symbolic representation – *ABILITY TO CREATE SYMBOLS TO REPRESENT SOMETHING NOT PRESENT*

symbols – *GESTURE, DRAWING OR WORD THAT REPRESENTS SOMETHING.*

signs – *TYPE OF MENTAL REPRESENTATION THAT'S SOCIALLY DEFINED & ACCEPED BY OTHER PEOPLE.*

symbolic play – *MAKE BELIEVE OR PRETEND GAMES*

animism – *ATTRIBUTING ANIMATE CHARACTERISTICS TO INANIMATE OBJECTS. (OCEAN IS ASLEEP)*

realism – *TO ATTRIBUTE REAL PHYSICAL PROPERTIES TO MENTAL ENTITIES (DREAM IS REAL)*

egocentrism – *INABILITY TO DISTINGUISH BETWEEN ONE'S OWN PERSPECTIVE & THAT OF ANOTHERS.*

egocentric speech — SPEECH WHEN PERSON IS ALONE OR NOT ATTEMPTING ᴧ TO COMMUNICATE.
irreversibility — CHILD'S INABILITY TO MENTALLY REVERSE HIS OR HER THINKING.
transductive reasoning — REASONING FROM THE PARTICULAR TO THE PARTICULAR.
classification — ABILITY TO SORT OBJECTS INTO CATEGORIES
phoneme — BASIC UNIT OF SOUND IN A LANGUAGE
morpheme — SMALLEST UNIT OF SOUND IN A GIVEN LANGUAGE.
syntax — RULES OF LANGUAGE — GRAMMAR
semantics — MEANINGS OF WORDS
pragmatics — RULES FOR USING LANGUAGE IN SOCIAL CONTEXT
overregulation — OVERUSE OF RULES OF LANGUAGE.
transformational rules — CHANGING SENTENCE STRUCTURE TO MAKE A QUESTION, NEGATION, ACTIVE, PASSIVE.

DEDUCTIVE REASONING — FROM GENERAL TO PARTICULAR.
INDUCTIVE " — " PARTICULAR TO GENERAL

REVIEW QUESTIONS

1. Briefly describe the physical development of the preschool child.

2. What advances in gross and fine motor coordination are made by the typical preschool child?

3. In Piaget's theory of cognitive development, what are the characteristics of the preoperational child?

4. Identify and explain five limitations of the preoperational thinker.

5. Describe the preoperational child's understanding of time, number, and the sorting of objects into classes.

6. In what ways does the preschool child's ability to process information differ from that of a school-age child?

7. What are the five components of language?

8. Briefly describe the process of language acquisition.

9. Name and briefly describe the major theories of language acquisition.

10. How do preschool and day-care programs affect the child's emotional, mental, and social development?

EXERCISES

1. Briefly describe the motor and manipulative skills of preschool children and the approximate age at which they are acquired.

GENERAL ABILITY	SPECIFIC ABILITY	AGE OF ONSET
Running		
Jumping		
Hopping		
Galloping		
Skipping		
Throwing		
Catching		
Kicking		
Striking		

2. Briefly summarize the three major theories of language acquisition.

THEORY	DESCRIPTION
Empirical approach	EMPHASIZES REINFORCEMENT & IMITATION SKINNER
Nativist approach	BORN W. INNATE TENDENCY TO ACQUIRE LANGUAGE. CHOMSKY
Cognitive approach	DIRECT RESULT OF COGNITIVE LEARNING PIAGET

QUIZ

True or False

_I_1. At 2 years of age the average child has quadrupled its birthweight.

_T_2. Much variation among children in physical growth is linked to ethnic origin.

_F_3. Later-born children tend to be taller than firstborn children.

_I_4. By the age of 5 a typical child is able to hop on either foot.

_F_5. Gross motor skills are more difficult for the preschool child to master than fine motor skills.

_F_6. During the preoperational stage, children's knowledge is limited to a here-and-now understanding of the objects and people with whom they interact.

_I_7. Symbols are mental representations that are unique to the child's own personal experiences.

_I_8. In symbolic play children often work out conflicts encountered in the real world.

_F_9. According to Piaget, children are able to distinguish between real and mental entities.

_F_10. Recent research has confirmed Piaget's claim that preschool children are unable to take another person's viewpoint.

_I_11. Preschool children are unable to shift attention from one detail or aspect of an event to another.

_F_12. Transductive reasoning involves reasoning from the particular to the general or from the general to the particular.

_I_13. Young children often confuse the concept of time with the concept of space.

_I_14. Piaget explained the child's understanding of number concepts as a special type of conservation.

_F_15. Inductive reasoning is the process of sorting objects into categories.

_I_16. Older children are able to look at an object longer than younger children.

_F_17. Information in long-term memory is available for about 30 seconds.

_F_18. The basic unit of sound is the morpheme.

_T_19. By age 6 children may know over 10,000 words.

58

F 20. A child's passive vocabulary consists of words that the child can say and use.

T 21. The term *telegraphic speech* refers to the two-word utterances of 2-year-olds.

F 22. Overregulation is the use of a single word to convey an entire thought.

T 23. Children begin using transformational rules around the age of 3 1/2.

F 24. The nativist approach to language acquisition emphasizes reinforcement and imitation as the basic processes for acquiring language skills.

T 25. According to Vygotsky, thought and language originate from two separate roots.

Sentence Completion

1. Children whose mothers _SMOKE_ during pregnancy are on the average 1/2 inch shorter than normal children.

2. By 2 years of age the child's brain weighs _75%_ of the brain's full adult weight.

3. Handedness appears to be determined by the child's _GENES_ or _PRENATAL ENVIRONMENT_ rather than _TRAINING_.

4. The ability to represent an event mentally is referred to as _SYMBOLIC FUNCTIONING_

5. Children's tendency to attribute feelings and intentions to objects that are not alive is known as _ANIMISM_

6. _EGOCENTRIC SPEECH_ is uttered either when children are alone or when they are with others but making no attempt to communicate their views to them.

7. _IRREVERSIBILITY_ refers to the child's inability to mentally reverse his or her thinking.

8. By the age of 2 a child can count _TWO_ objects.

9. Preschoolers use gross _PERCEPTUAL_ features to judge number.

10. Preschool children often group objects together on a _THEMATIC_ basis.

11. Before the age of 4, children do not have _STRATEGIES_ for remembering things.

12. A word is an example of a _MORPHEME_

13. _SEMANTICS_ refers to the rules governing the meaning of words and sentences.

14. The infant begins to understand words at the age of _6 MONTHS_.

15. The tendency of young children to use words in an overrestrictive fashion is known as _UNDEREXTENSION_.

16. The grammatical rules of a language are its _SYNTAX_.

17. _TRANSFORMATIONAL_ rules allow the child to translate the basic meaning of a sentence into a grammatically correct sentence.

18. The _EMPIRICAL_ approach to language acquisition emphasizes reinforcement and imitation as the basic processes for acquiring language skills.

19. _INTERACTIONISTS_ focus on the ways in which children learn the rules of their language.

20. Compared to monolingual children, bilingual children have _SMALLER_ vocabularies in both languages.

21. In the United States over _1 MILLION_ preschool children attend some form of nursery school.

22. _HEAD START_ programs are designed to provide preschool-age children with experiences that they are deprived of in their home environments.

23. Most studies have found that day care _DOES NOT_ (does/does not) disrupt the child's emotional bond to the mother.

24. The results of many studies show that day-care children interact _MORE_ with their peers than home-reared children do.

25. High-quality day-care programs are characterized by a _LOW_ child-to-adult ratio, day-care workers who are trained in _CHILD HOOD EDUCATION_; and _RESPONSIVE_ day-care workers.

Multiple Choice

_D_ 1. Between birth and the age of 2, the average child increases in height by
   a. 25 percent.
   b. one-third.
   c. 50 percent.
   (d.) two-thirds.

_A_ 2. At age 5, compared to children whose mothers did not smoke during pregnancy those whose mothers smoked are
   (a.) about 1/2 inch shorter.
   b. about an inch shorter.
   c. about the same height.
   d. slightly taller.

_C_ 3. Which of the following statements is *not* true?
   a. Between the ages of 2 and 6 the child becomes increasingly co-ordinated.
   b. During the preschool years the child's leg and arm joints become more susceptible to injury.
   (c.) The preschool child has difficulty starting and stopping movements.
   d. Spills and falls become less frequent between the ages of 2 and 5.

B 4. At what age does the child begin to run?
    a.   1 1/2 years
    b.   2-3 years
    c.   4-5 years
    d.   5 1/2 years

C 5. The preschooler's skill in fine motor skills results from
    a.   maturation of the nervous system.
    b.   experience manipulating objects.
    c.   both a and b.
    d.   neither a nor b.

B 6. Imitation of actions in the absence of a model is referred to as
    a.   symbolic play.
    b.   deferred imitation.
    c.   egocentric speech.
    d.   transductive reasoning.

B 7. The word *orthodontist* is an example of a
    a.   symbol.
    b.   sign.
    c.   phoneme.
    d.   morpheme.

A 8. Children's tendency to attribute feelings and intentions to objects that are not alive is referred to as
    a.   animism.
    b.   egocentrism.
    c.   realism.
    d.   centration.

D 9. Which of the following is a limitation on the preoperational child's thought?
    a.   egocentrism
    b.   centration
    c.   irreversibility
    d.   all of the above

C 10. Centration in the thinking of preschool children refers to
    a.   speech in which the child makes no attempt to communicate his or her views to others.
    b.   reliance on physical objects or events that the child can manipulate mentally.
    c.   the tendency to focus attention on one detail or aspect of an event.
    d.   the child's inability to mentally reverse his or her thinking.

D 11. One rainy day the mail was delivered late, and Jimmy concluded that the mail is always late on rainy days. This is an example of
    a.   inductive reasoning.
    b.   deductive reasoning.
    c.   conductive reasoning.
    d.   transductive reasoning.

D 12. Which of the following statements is *not* true?
   a.   Preschool children often confuse the concept of time with the concept of space.
   b.   In telling time, preschool children are dependent on the spatial arrangement of the numbers on the clock.
   c.   Children begin using words for time in the preschool years.
   d.   Beginning at age 5, the child understands that objects can move over unequal distances in the same amount of time.

A 13. Preschool children judge number by
   a.   relying on perceptual features.
   b.   counting.
   c.   matching objects in different rows.
   d.   none of the above.

C 14. A class of objects consisting of a red sock, a blue shirt, and a green tie is an example of
   a.   overextension.
   b.   overregulation.
   c.   a taxonomic category.
   d.   a spurious category.

A 15. The ability to identify a stimulus that one has seen before is termed
   a.   recognition memory.
   b.   recall memory.
   c.   short-term memory.
   d.   long-term memory.

B 16. The smallest unit of _meaningful_ sound in a language is a
   a.   phoneme.
   b.   morpheme.
   c.   word.
   d.   sentence.

D 17. The rules for using a language in a social context are referred to as
   a.   syntax.
   b.   semantics.
   c.   grammar.
   d.   pragmatics.

C 18. By the age of 3 the average child has a vocabulary of over
   a.   200 words.
   b.   400 words.
   c.   800 words.
   d.   1000 words.

B 19. A holophrase is
   a.   a form of "telegraphic speech."
   b.   a single word that conveys an entire thought.
   c.   a rule for creating a grammatically correct sentence.
   d.   a rule for using language in a social context.

_A_ 20. The rule in French that requires the use of *ne* and *pas* in a negative statement is an example of a
  a. transformational rule.
  b. morphological rule.
  c. pragmatic rule.
  d. all of the above.

_B_ 21. The empirical approach to language acquisition
  a. views language development as a natural consequence of physical maturation.
  b. emphasizes reinforcement and imitation as the basic processes for acquiring language skills.
  c. focuses on the ways in which children learn the rules of their language.
  d. views language as a direct result of cognitive development.

_C_ 22. Which of the following theorists maintains that humans are born with an innate tendency to acquire language?
  a. B. F. Skinner
  b. Jean Piaget
  c. Noam Chomsky
  d. Eric Lenneberg

_D_ 23. Which of the following statements is true?
  a. Bilingual children have lower cognitive abilities than monolingual children.
  b. Bilingual children are less flexible in their use of labels for words than monolingual children.
  c. Monolingual children are more creative storytellers than bilingual children.
  d. None of the above.

_A_ 24. Which of the following generally offers a program of educational enrichment on a basis usually limited to three to five half-days a week?
  a. nursery schools
  b. family day-care programs
  c. day-care centers
  d. none of the above

_C_ 25. Which of the following statements is *not* true?
  a. Day care has been found not to disrupt the child's emotional bond to the mother.
  b. Good-quality nonmaternal care does not appear to affect the child's intellectual functioning.
  c. Day-care children interact less with their peers than do home-raised children.
  d. Children who attend high-quality day-care centers have been found to be more compliant than children enrolled in low-quality day care.

Matching

A. Limitations on the preoperational child's thought processes:

D 1. Centration
C 2. Transductive reasoning
A 3. Egocentrism
B 4. Irreversibility
E 5. Concreteness

a. The child believes that other people see the world the same way he or she does.
b. The child is unable to go back to the point of origin of a thought.
c. The child reasons from the particular to the particular.
d. The child focuses on one aspect of an event.
e. The child relies on physical objects or events that can be mentally manipulated.

B. Components of language:

B 1. Syntax
C 2. Phonemes
D 3. Semantics
E 4. Pragmatics
A 5. Morphemes

a. The smallest units of meaningful sound.
b. The rules by which words are combined to form larger units.
c. The basic units of sound in a language.
d. The rules governing the meaning of words and sentences.
e. The rules for using a language in a social context.

C. Theoretical approaches to language acquisition:

B 1. Cognitive
A 2. Nativist
C 3. Empirical

a. The child has an innate ability to acquire language skills.
b. The ability to mentally represent actions is basic to acquiring language skills.
c. Reinforcement and imitation are the basic processes for acquiring language skills.

ANSWERS

True or False

1. T
2. T
3. F
4. T
5. F
6. F

7. T
8. T
9. F
10. F
11. T
12. F
13. T
14. T
15. F
16. T
17. F
18. F
19. T
20. F
21. T
22. F
23. T
24. F
25. T

Sentence Completion

1. smoked
2. 75
3. genes, prenatal environment, training
4. symbolic functioning
5. animism
6. egocentric speech
7. irreversibility
8. two
9. perceptual
10. thematic
11. strategies
12. morpheme
13. semantics
14. six months
15. underextension
16. syntax
17. transformational
18. empirical
19. interactionists
20. smaller
21. 1 million
22. Head Start
23. does not
24. more
25. low, childhood education, responsive/affectionate/stimulating

Multiple Choice

1. d
2. a
3. c
4. b
5. c
6. b
7. b
8. a
9. d
10. c
11. d
12. d
13. a
14. c
15. a
16. b
17. d
18. c
19. b
20. a
21. b
22. c
23. d
24. a
25. c

Matching

A. 1. d
   2. c
   3. a
   4. b
   5. e

B. 1. b
   2. c
   3. d
   4. e
   5. a

C. 1. b
   2. a
   3. c

Chapter 6

PRESCHOOL YEARS: PERSONALITY AND SOCIAL DEVELOPMENT

CHAPTER OUTLINE

The Development of Self
    Self-Concept Defined
    Erikson's Stage of Initiative vs. Guilt
    Identification
    Gender-Role Typing
        Gender Identity
        Gender Roles
        Gender Differences
        Gender-Role Socialization
The Child in the Family
    Parenting Role
    Parenting Styles
    Encouraging Compliance
        Punishment
        Alternatives to Punishment
    The Changing Family
        Maternal Employment
        Divorce
        Single-Parent Families
        Stepparent Families
    Child Abuse
        Incidence
        Causes
        Effects
        Treatment
        Sexual Abuse
The Child's Social World
    Aggression
    Prosocial Behavior
        Empathy
        Altruism
    Social Play
        Early Play
        Types of Play

SUMMARY OF KEY CONCEPTS

1. The child's self-concept develops gradually between ages 2 and 6 through numerous social interactions and includes gender identity and the development of gender-appropriate behaviors.

2. According to Erikson, preschool children experience a crisis in which initiative is counteracted by guilt. Overcritical reactions to a young child's initiative can lead to intense feelings of guilt.

3. Through the process of identification children take on characteristics of their parents. Gender-appropriate behaviors are learned through observation of models and reinforcement.

4. Within the family, parents socialize children by disciplining them for exhibiting inappropriate behaviors and reinforcing them for exhibiting desirable ones. Four styles of parenting have been observed: authoritarian, authoritative, permissive, and uninvolved.

5. Discipline includes the use of punishment when children do not obey parents' directives. Punishment is most effective when it is applied consistently and accompanied by a rationale.

6. In families in which the mother is employed outside the home, the children benefit from a more flexible female role model. Single-parent families experience a variety of stresses that affect parent-child relationships. Stepfamilies face the added difficulty of adjusting to different family rules and new parenting styles.

7. Child abuse is a serious problem, often caused by stresses that overburden the caregiver's ability to cope with the demands of children. Treatment of child abuse entails providing abusive families with community support and reeducation. In cases of sexual abuse, children are taught to say no to anyone who seeks to touch them in sexual ways.

8. Young children often display physical aggression in their play activity, but by age 6 the frequency of aggression decreases as the child acquires self-control and alternative ways of dealing with frustration.

9. Prosocial behavior develops as the child becomes aware of other people's feelings. Parents can encourage sharing, helping, and other prosocial behaviors by providing examples and expressing disapproval of actions that cause distress to others.

10. Social play develops in four stages: solitary play, parallel play, associative play, and cooperative play.

KEY TERMS AND PHRASES

socialization – *PROCESS BY WHICH CHILD LEARNS EXPECTED BEHAVIORS OF A CULTURE OR GROUP*
self-concept – *THE WAY A PERSON VIEWS HIMSELF.*
identification – *PROCESS BY WHICH CHILD TAKES ON BELIEFS OF ANOTHER.*
gender identity – *RECOGNITION & ACCEPTANCE OF ONE'S OWN GENDER.*
gender typing – *PROCESS BY WHICH CHILDREN ACQUIRE CULTURALLY EXPECTED BEHAVIORS.*
gender constancy – *RECOGNITION THAT ONE'S GENDER DOESN'T CHANGE.*
gender roles – *PATTERN OF BEHAVIORS CONSIDERED APPROPRIAT WITHIN A CULTURE*
discipline – *STRATEGY PARENTS USE TO GET CHILDREN TO COMPLY W. RULES.*
time out – *REMOVING PERSON FROM SETTING IN WHICH BEHAVIOR TO BE CHANGED IS REINFORCED.*
reconstituted family – *FAMILY CREATED THRO' REMARRIAGE OF ADULTS W. CHILDREN*

REVIEW QUESTIONS

1. What is meant by personality? By self-concept?

2. What is gender identity? How do children develop gender identity?

3. Are differences in gender roles related to biologically based differences in behavior, or are they learned?

4. List the four parenting styles that have been identified by researchers.

5. Is physical punishment effective as a means of changing undesirable behavior? What alternatives are available for dealing with such behavior?

6. What effects, if any, does maternal employment have on the development of the child?

7. Briefly describe the impact of divorce on younger and older children.

8. What special problems confront single-parent and stepparent families?

9. What factors contribute to the incidence of child abuse?

10. Distinguish between instrumental and hostile aggression.

EXERCISES

1. Briefly describe the four parenting styles that have been identified by researchers.

PARENTING STYLE	DESCRIPTION
Authoritarian	
Permissive	
Authoritative	
Uninvolved	

2. Briefly describe the stages in the development of social play.

STAGE	DESCRIPTION
1. Solitary play	
2. Parallel play	
3. Associative play	
4. Cooperative play	

QUIZ

True or False

_T_ 1. Socialization is the process of learning how to get along with other groups of people.

_F_ 2. The child's self-concept emerges rather suddenly around the age of 4.

_F_ 3. According to Erikson, the crisis faced by the child in the preschool years is an identity crisis.

_T_ 4. Children become aware of gender as a dimension on which to classify people between the ages of 2 and 3.

_F_ 5. Gender constancy must be achieved before a child can acquire a sense of gender identity.

_F_ 6. Gender roles are universal patterns of behaviors considered appropriate for males and females.

_T_ 7. Maccoby and Jacklin found only four behavioral differences that can be attributed to gender alone.

_T_ 8. There are no gender differences in mathematical ability during the childhood years.

_F_ 9. Parental stereotyping of children on the basis of gender has increased dramatically in recent years.

_T_ 10. Play with gender-stereotyped toys is one of the earliest manifestations of gender typing.

_F_ 11. Gender-role behavior is fixed by the time the individual reaches adolescence.

_F_ 12. The term *discipline* refers to severe punishment bordering on child abuse.

_T_ 13. An authoritarian parent believes that the child should accept the parent's word without question.

_F_ 14. An uninvolved parent believes that the parent should behave in an affirmative, acceptant, and benign manner toward the child's impulses and actions.

_T_ 15. The most effective form of discipline occurs when parents are consistent in the use of rationally based demands.

_T_ 16. "Time out" is a technique used by parents to deal with disruptive and inappropriate behavior.

_F_ 17. Today about 50 percent of households in the United States are single-parent families.

_T_ 18. Researchers have found no difference between employed and nonemployed mothers in amount of contact with their preschool children.

_T_ 19. Each year about a million children experience the divorce of their parents.

_F_ 20. After a divorce, children's primary concern is whether their parents will marry other people.

_F_ 21. Unlike younger children, adolescents are not affected by divorce.

_T_ 22. It has been estimated that four out of ten children born in the 1970s will spend some time in a single-parent family.

_F_ 23. The remarriage of adults with children creates a traditional family.

_T_ 24. Child abuse is especially likely to occur in families with many children.

_F_ 25. In the majority of incest cases the offender is the biological father.

Sentence Completion

1. Between the ages of 2 and 6, children learn behaviors that allow them to become _MEMBERS OF A GROUP._

2. _PERSONALITY_ generally refers to the characteristic way in which a person behaves.

3. According to Erikson, the preschool child must resolve the developmental crisis of _INITIATIVE_ versus _GUILT_

4. _IDENTIFICATION_ is the process by which a child takes on the beliefs, desires, and values of another person.

5. Gender expectations vary according to the _CULTURE_ and _TIME PERIOD_ in which children are raised.

6. _GENDER CONSTANCY_ is achieved when the child comes to believe that boys always grow up to be men and girls always grow up to be women.

7. Maccoby and Jacklin found that males and females differ in _AGGRESSION_ and certain _COGNITIVE_ skills. _& INTELLECTUAL_

8. There is no evidence to support the view that girls are more _SOCIABLE_ or more _SUGGESTIBLE_ than boys.

9. One of the earliest manifestations of gender typing is play with _GENDER, STEREOTYPED TOYS._

10. In addition to influencing the child's self-concept, gender-differentiated socialization has a profound impact on _COGNITIVE DEVELOPMENT_

11. _DISCIPLINE_ refers to parents' strategies for eliciting compliance to their authority.

12. The three basic styles of parenting that have been identified by researchers are _PERMISSIVE_, _AUTHORITARIAN_, and _AUTHORITATIVE_.

13. Other researchers have identified a fourth parenting style, _UNINVOLVED_, in which the parent is indifferent to the child's need for discipline or affection.

14. Children who are harshly punished at home are more likely to be _AGGRESSIVE_ with other children and teachers.

15. Parents who use _proactive_ controls avoid potential conflict by distracting their children before the disruptive behavior begins.

16. In the last decade, over _50_ percent of married mothers of school-age children were employed.

17. Adolescents whose mothers work outside the home receive more encouragement to be _independent_

18. The primary reaction of children to divorce is _anger_.

19. Immediately following a divorce fathers usually have _more_ contact with their children than they did before the divorce.

20. Child abuse includes _physical_ or _emotional_ injury, _sexual_ abuse, and _negligent_ treatment or mistreatment of children under the age of 18 by adults entrusted with their care.

21. Over half of all incidents of child abuse appear to have begun as a _disciplinary action_ that got out of control.

22. The most effective way of treating child abuse is by _preventing future incidents_.

23. The victim of incest is usually a _female child_

24. _instrumental_ aggressive behaviors are designed to accomplish an end.

25. The first step in the development of prosocial behavior begins when the child is able to _empathize_ with another person.

Multiple Choice

_B_ 1. The process by which children learn behaviors that allow them to become members of a group is termed
   a. gender-role training.
   b. socialization.
   c. psychosexual development.
   d. conditioning.

_C_ 2. Young children first define themselves in terms of their
   a. personality traits.
   b. gender.
   c. activities.
   d. feelings.

72

C 3. According to Erik Erikson, between the ages of 3 and 6 children must resolve issues related to
   a. trust versus mistrust.
   b. autonomy versus shame and doubt.
   c. initiative versus guilt.
   d. identity versus role confusion.

A 4. The process by which a child takes on the beliefs, desires, and values of another person is known as
   a. identification.
   b. empathy.
   c. modeling.
   d. imitation.

D 5. Children who tease a boy for wearing a necklace to school illustrate
   a. gender identity.
   b. gender constancy.
   c. gender sensitivity.
   d. gender typing.

B 6. Children's gender identity is established by the age of
   a. 1.
   b. 3.
   c. 4 or 5.
   d. 7.

C 7. In modern cultures gender roles are becoming more
   a. clearly defined.
   b. narrowly defined.
   c. flexible.
   d. none of the above; they have disappeared.

D 8. There is some evidence of biologically based gender differences in
   a. aggression.
   b. visual-spatial ability.
   c. verbal ability.
   d. all of the above.

C 9. Which of the following statements is *not* true?
   a. Preschool children are rewarded for gender-appropriate behavior.
   b. One of the earliest manifestations of gender typing is play with gender-stereotyped toys.
   c. Gender-role training systematically requires females to engage in more problem-solving activities than males.
   d. Gender-role behavior undergoes change throughout the lifespan.

D 10. Child-rearing practices are determined by
   a. the culture in which the child is raised.
   b. the parents' experience.
   c. the nature of the child.
   d. all of the above.

73

_b_ 11. A parent who values obedience and favors forceful measures to curb self-will is described as
    a.   authoritative.
    (b) authoritarian.
    c.   permissive.
    d.   uninvolved.

_A_ 12. A parent who believes children should be free from restraint as much as is consistent with survival is described as
    (a) permissive.
    b.   uninvolved.
    c.   authoritative.
    d.   authoritarian.

_A_ 13. The most effective form of discipline for children occurs when parents are
    (a) consistent.
    b.   forceful.
    c.   uninvolved.
    d.   abusive.

_b_ 14. Instead of being punished, a misbehaving child may be removed from the setting in which the behavior occurs. This procedure is known as
    a.   prosocial behavior.
    (b) time out.
    c.   proactive control.
    d.   none of the above.

_c_ 15. About 20 percent of the households in the United States are
    a.   extended families.
    b.   reconstituted families.
    (c) single-parent families.
    d.   traditional nuclear families.

_A_ 16. Which of the following statements is *not* true?
    (a.) Children whose mothers are not employed receive better care than those whose mothers are employed.
    b.   The quantity of care a child receives from its mother does not affect the child's development.
    c.   Children whose mothers are employed have a less stereotyped view of female gender roles.
    d.   Children of employed mothers have more training in independence than children of nonemployed mothers.

_D_ 17. Immediately after a divorce the biggest concern of children is
    a.   which parent was at fault.
    b.   whether their parents will remarry.
    c.   how their peers will react.
    (d.) what will happen to them.

_B_ 18. The impact of divorce is greatest for
    a. infants.
    (b.) preschool children.
    c. older children.
    d. adolescents.

_A_ 19. Which of the following statements is *not* true?
    (a.) Children in single-parent families are less responsible and independent than children in two-parent families.
    b. Most single-parent families in the United States are headed by women.
    c. The most significant characteristic of single-parent families is that they are economically stressed.
    d. Single-parent families receive less social or community support than two-parent families.

_D_ 20. A reconstituted family is one in which
    a. grandparents and other relatives are part of the household.
    b. the parents are divorced but have joint custody of the children.
    c. the parents have been reconciled after a separation.
    (d.) one or both parents have children from previous marriages.

_D_ 21. Which of the following is *not* included in the definition of child abuse?
    a. incest
    b. emotional injury
    c. negligent treatment
    (d.) corporal punishment

_B_ 22. Which of the following are at risk for child abuse?
    a. families in which the mother is employed
    (b.) families that are experiencing economic strains
    c. single-child families
    d. female-headed families

_B_ 23. In two-thirds of incest cases the offender is
    a. the father.
    (b.) the stepfather.
    c. a stranger.
    d. a woman.

_A_ 24. Behaviors that are intended to harm or hurt another person are referred to as
    (a.) hostile aggression.
    b. instrumental aggression.
    c. prosocial behavior.
    d. antisocial behavior.

_____25. In which of the following do two or three children use the same equipment, each in his or her own way?
   a. solitary play
   b. parallel play
   c. associative play
   d. cooperative play

Matching

A. Gender-related concepts:

_A_ 1. Gender typing

_D_ 2. Gender identity

_B_ 3. Gender roles

_C_ 4. Gender constancy

   a. Incorporation into personality of cultural expectations based on biological gender.
   b. A set of behaviors considered appropriate for women or men.
   c. The realization that a person's gender does not change.
   d. Recognition and acceptance of oneself as male or female.

B. Parenting styles:

_A_ 1. Authoritarian

_C_ 2. Permissive

_B_ 3. Authoritative

   a. Parents believe in restricting the child's autonomy.
   b. Parents encourage verbal give-and-take.
   c. Parents behave in a benign manner toward the child's impulses and actions.

C. Stages in the development of social play:

_D_ 1. Solitary play

_B_ 2. Parallel play

_A_ 3. Associative play

_C_ 4. Cooperative play

   a. Children play in small groups but participate in their own way.
   b. Children play within earshot of a peer.
   c. Children play with others and share playthings.
   d. Children play with toys within earshot of their parents.

ANSWERS

True or False

1. T
2. F
3. F
4. T
5. F
6. F
7. T
8. T
9. F
10. T
11. F
12. F
13. T
14. F
15. T
16. T
17. F
18. T
19. T
20. F
21. F
22. T
23. F
24. T
25. F

Sentence Completion

1. members of a group
2. personality
3. initiative, guilt
3. identification
5. culture, time period
6. gender constancy
7. aggression, cognitive/intellectual
8. sociable, suggestible
9. gender-stereotyped toys
10. cognitive development
11. discipline
12. permissive, authoritarian, authoritative
13. uninvolved
14. aggressive
15. proactive
16. 50
17. independent
18. anger
19. more
20. physical, emotional, sexual, negligent
21. disciplinary action
22. preventing future incidents
23. female child
24. instrumental
25. empathize

Multiple Choice

1. b
2. c
3. c
4. a
5. d
6. b
7. c
8. d
9. c
10. d
11. b
12. a
13. a
14. b
15. c
16. a
17. d
18. b
19. a
20. d
21. d
22. b
23. b
24. a
25. c

Matching

A. 1. a
   2. d
   3. b
   4. c

77

B. 1. a
    2. c
    3. b

C. 1. d
    2. b
    3. a
    4. c

Chapter 7

MIDDLE CHILDHOOD:
PHYSICAL GROWTH, COGNITION, AND LEARNING

CHAPTER OUTLINE

Physical Growth
    Size and Proportion
    Motor Development
    Physical Fitness
Cognitive Growth
    Piaget's Theory: Concrete Operational Thought
        Decentration and Reversibility
        Conservation Skills
        Classification Skills
        Children's Humor
    Perspective Taking and Social Cognition
    Moral Reasoning
        Piaget's Views
        Kohlberg's Theory
        Evaluating Kohlberg's Theory
        Training Moral Behavior
Information Processing
    Attention
    Memory
        Strategies
    Cognitive Styles
        Field Dependence--Field Independence
        Impulsivity--Reflection
Assessment of Mental Capabilities
    IQ Tests
        Interpreting IQ Scores
Learning Disabilities
    Characteristics
    Causes
    Treatment

SUMMARY OF KEY CONCEPTS

1. During middle childhood children grow taller and leaner, and their fine and gross motor coordination improves. Physical fitness and skills contribute to the child's self-concept.

2. According to Piaget, children enter the stage of *concrete operations* at age 6 or 7. Conservation and classification skills develop throughout the period from age 6 to age 12.

3. Children's appreciation of humor is closely linked to their level of cognitive development. Being able to understand and tell a joke adds to children's sense of competence.

4. During the concrete-operational period children lose their egocentric perspective and become able to consider other viewpoints besides their own. *Social cognition* refers to the child's awareness of other people and understanding of their motives.

5. Piaget described three stages in the development of moral reasoning: premoral judgment, moral realism, and autonomous reasoning. Piaget's early work was refined by Lawrence Kohlberg, who identified three levels and six stages of morality.

6. In middle childhood children become more capable of processing information about the world. Their attention span increases and they are less easily distracted. Their memory skills increase as they make more efficient use of memory strategies.

7. Children develop their own ways of processing information and solving problems. Three *cognitive styles* that have been studied are field dependence-independence and impulsivity-reflection.

8. The IQ test was developed to predict school performance. Two popular standardized tests are the Stanford-Binet and the Wechsler IQ series. IQ tests have been criticized for being too narrowly constructed and for embodying race, sex, and class biases.

9. Some children have difficulty learning certain subjects in school. Although the causes of such *learning disabilities* are not well understood, psychologists and teachers recognize the value of early diagnosis and treatment.

KEY TERMS AND PHRASES

physical fitness — OPTIMAL FUNCTIONING OF BODY MEASURED BY MUSCULAR STRENGTH, HEART RATE, LUNG CAPACITY

concrete operations — 3rd Stage - Piaget - logical tho't & ability to manipulate symbols

formal operations — 4th Stage - Piaget's

Piaget — decentration — shift of attention Adolescence - ABSTRACT, HYPOTHETICAL REASONING

" — reversibility — Think backward, from one perceptual attribute

" — horizontal decalage — CHILDREN ACQUIRE CONSERVATION OF DIFFERENT PHYSICAL to another.

social cognition CHARACTERISTICS AT DIFFERENT AGES.

moral reasoning

moral behavior

encoding — MEMORY PROCESS WHERE INFO IS STORED USING CUES WHICH ARE LATER USED FOR RECALL.

retrieval — ABILITY TO REMOVE INFO FROM LONG TERM MEMORY.

mnemonic devices — STRATEGY FOR RECALLING INFO FROM SHORT OR LONG TERM MEMORY.

cognitive style — A PERSON'S PARTICULAR PATTERN OF THO'T &

mental age — BEHAVIOR USED TO RESPOND TO COGNITIVE TASKS.

HIGHEST AGE LEVEL AT/FOR WHICH PERSON PASSES MUST ITEMS ON IQ TEST.

intelligence quotient — MEASURE OF PERSON'S INTELLECTUAL CAPABILITIES
learning disability — PROBLEM INVOLVING ONE OR MORE OF BASIC PROCESSES
dyslexia — INABILITY TO READ   NECESSARY TO UNDERSTAND LANGUAGE & NUMBERS.
dysgraphia — " TO TRANSFER AS A RESULT OF DIFFICULTY IN COMBINING INFO FROM
dyscalcula — " TO MENTALLY IDEAS OR SOUNDS INTO   DIFFERENT SENSORY AVENUES.
minimal brain damage   MANIPULATE NUMBERS. WRITTEN WORDS,

REVIEW QUESTIONS

1. Briefly characterize physical growth in middle childhood.

2. What is meant by physical fitness? What are its implications for development?

3. What stage of cognitive development do children enter at the age of 6 or 7?

4. List the stages in the development of conservation.

5. What is the significance of children's understanding of humor?

6. List the stages of moral reasoning identified by Piaget and Kohlberg.

7. Briefly describe the advances in information processing that occur in middle childhood.

8. Name two cognitive styles that have been studied by psychologists.

9. What kinds of tests are used to assess mental capacities? What are some criticisms of those tests?

10. Briefly describe three common types of learning disabilities.

EXERCISES

1. Briefly describe the methods used to test conservation and the child's response.

TYPE	METHOD	RESPONSE	AGE
Liquid			
Number			
Length			
Area			
Matter			
Volume			

2. Compare Piaget and Kohlberg's theories of moral reasoning.

STAGE	PIAGET	KOHLBERG
1.		
2.		
3.		

QUIZ

<u>True or False</u>

F 1. During middle childhood children tend to make large spurts in height and weight.

T 2. Urban children tend to be taller and heavier than rural children.

T 3. Popularity in middle childhood is linked to physical fitness.

F 4. The transition from prelogical to logical thought occurs at about age 4.

F 5. Reversibility is the ability to shift attention from one perceptual attribute to another.

T 6. The idea that children acquire conservation of different characteristics at different ages is referred to as horizontal decalage.

F 7. Usually, the last aspect of conservation achieved by the child is conservation of area.

T 8. During the concrete-operational period children are able to coordinate the properties of class intension and class extension.

T 9. The essential feature of a joke is incongruity.

F 10. The concrete-operational child is characterized by an egocentric perspective.

F 11. Social cognition is the final stage in the development of moral reasoning.

F 12. The stage in which rules are regarded as sacred and unchangeable is referred to as the universal ethnical principles stage.

T 13. Kohlberg proposed that moral reasoning develops in a sequence of six stages.

T 14. Preconventional morality generally predominates during middle childhood.

F 15. Recent research has confirmed that Kohlberg's levels of moral development are universal.

T 16. Children can be trained to take the role of another person.

F 17. Children tend to become more distractible with age.

F 18. Clustering is a coding strategy for storing and retrieving information.

T 19. The Embedded Figures Test is used to assess an individual's ability to separate out a relevant feature from its context.

F 20. The Matching Familiar Figures test is used to test field dependence-independence.

T 21. A child's intelligence quotient can be calculated by dividing mental age by chronological age and multiplying by 100.

T 22. The Wechsler intelligence tests assess verbal and performance skills.

F 23. IQ tests have been criticized because they do not adequately reflect what the child has already learned.

F 24. Dyskinesia is a learning disability that results in inability to read or spell.

_T_ 25. The difficulties in academic performance found among learning-disabled children are not a result of mental deficiency.

Sentence Completion

1. The period from age 6 to age 12 is known as _middle childhood_.

2. Between the ages of 6 and 8 the _myelination_ of neurons nears completion.

3. _Phys. fitness_ refers to the body's optimal level of functioning.

4. The stage of _concrete operations_ is characterized by the acquisition of conceptual skills that permit logical manipulation of symbols.

5. The acquisition of _conservation_ allows children to make logical predictions about what will happen to physical objects with which they come into contact.

6. Concrete-operational children are able to coordinate the properties of class _intension_ and class _extension_.

7. The pleasure of a joke comes from _figuring it out_.

8. Taking the viewpoint of others is closely related to the comprehension and use of _relational_ terms.

9. _Moral reasoning_ refers to a person's judgments about the appropriateness of an action based on some set of rules.

10. According to Piaget, by about 10 years of age children enter a stage of moral reasoning known as _autonomous morality_.

11. Kohlberg was most interested not in the answers to moral dilemmas but in the _reasoning behind the answers_.

12. Children between the ages of 4 and 10 seem to function at the _preconventional_ level of moral reasoning.

13. According to Carol Gilligan, Kohlberg's ideas are based on a _male_ perspective on morality.

14. Parents who provide children with _clear_ and _direct_ instructions about the appropriateness of their actions are more likely to encourage moral behavior.

15. As children grow older they become more _selective_ in the way they direct their attentional resources.

16. Two frequently used memory strategies are _chunking_ and _clustering_.

17. When presented with a problem, some children respond in a quick, cursory, and inaccurate manner, a style that is labeled _impulsive_.

18. The first practical test to measure the mental capabilities of schoolchildren was published in 1905 by ___*Binet*___

19. A child's score on the Stanford-Binet or Wechsler test is translated into an IQ score by comparing the child's performance with the ___*standardized group performance*___

20. IQ tests have been criticized for placing too much emphasis on ___*verbal*___ and ___*logical*___ cognitive skills.

21. When used correctly, IQ scores help predict ___*school achievement*___.

22. Difficulty in writing is termed ___*dysgraphia*___

23. Children with undiagnosed learning disabilities often develop ___*behavior*___ problems.

24. One explanation of learning disabilities is that these difficulties are a result of a ___*developmental*___ lag.

25. It is important to diagnose learning disabilities early enough in the child's schooling to prevent the buildup of ___*frustration*___ and loss of ___*self esteem*___ from poor perform-ance.

Multiple Choice

A 1. During middle childhood children's growth becomes
    a. more uniform.
    b. more erratic.
    c. minimal.
    d. unpredictable.

A 2. Which of the following statements is *not* true?
    a. By age 12 boys are two years ahead of girls in height and weight.
    b. Boys have greater forearm strength than girls.
    c. Girls typically lose their teeth earlier than boys.
    d. Heredity seems to account for most differences among children in size.

D 3. Compared to children in the 1960s, children today are
    a. more intelligent.
    b. less intelligent.
    c. more physically fit.
    d. less physically fit.

B 4. Researchers have found that the least popular children are
    a. normal in weight and obedient.
    b. normal in weight and disobedient.
    c. obese and obedient.
    d. obese and disobedient.

_B_ 5. At the age of 6 or 7 children make the transition to
   a. prelogical thought.
   b. logical thought.
   c. abstract thought.
   d. conventional thought.

_C_ 6. A child who can judge the amounts of liquid in glasses of different sizes has acquired the ability to
   a. conserve volume.
   b. reverse thought.
   c. decenter.
   d. classify.

_C_ 7. The term *horizontal decalage* refers to
   a. the ability to mentally retrace actions in thought.
   b. the ability to define a class and list all the members of that class.
   c. the idea that children acquire conservation of different characteristics at different ages.
   d. the idea that children acquire aspects of concrete-operational thought in the same invariant order.

_D_ 8. Which of the following is a cognitive competence that is acquired during the stage of concrete operations?
   a. decentration
   b. reversibility
   c. class extension
   d. all of the above

_B_ 9. To be funny, a joke must be
   a. obvious.
   b. moderately complex.
   c. challenging.
   d. able to fool the listener.

_A_ 10. Knowledge about social relationships and reactions is called
   a. social cognition.
   b. decentration.
   c. moral reasoning.
   d. egocentric thinking.

_C_ 11. In Piaget's theory of development, the first stage is
   a. autonomous morality.
   b. instrumental exchange orientation.
   c. premoral judgment.
   d. law and order morality.

_C_ 12. According to Piaget, at what age do children begin to realize that rules are made by people?
    a.   3
    b.   6
    c.   10
    d.   13

_B_ 13. According to Kohlberg, at what stage of moral development do children conform to rules to gain approval?
    a.   preconventional
    b.   conventional
    c.   postconventional
    d.   none of the above

_D_ 14. Kohlberg's views have been challenged by critics who claim that
    a.   they are based on a male perspective on morality.
    b.   they cannot be considered universal.
    c.   they are based on moral standards held in the United States.
    d.   all of the above.

_C_ 15. Which of the following statements is *not* true?
    a.   Children must have the ability to reason before they can act morally.
    b.   Highly critical disciplinary actions are likely to discourage moral growth.
    c.   Children cannot be trained to take the role of another person.
    d.   Adults can facilitate moral development by rewarding desired behavior and punishing undesired behavior.

_A_ 16. Which of the following statements is true?
    a.   As they get older, children become more attentive to specific sources of information.
    b.   As they get older, children become less selective in the way they direct their attentional resources.
    c.   Children's capacity for memory does not change significantly in middle childhood.
    d.   Preschool children are especially likely to use verbal rehearsal as a memory strategy.

_D_ 17. Strategies to aid recall are known as
    a.   retrieval strategies.
    b.   metamemory.
    c.   categorization styles.
    d.   mnemonic devices.

_A_ 18. An 8-year-old knows that it is easier to remember a series of numbers when they are grouped. This is an example of
    a.   chunking.
    b.   encoding.
    c.   retrieval.
    d.   clustering.

B 19. People who are field dependent
   a. respond to a problem in a quick, cursory, and inaccurate manner.
   b. have difficulty separating out a relevant feature from the context in which it is embedded.
   c. withhold answers until they have carefully evaluated their ideas.
   d. group objects together on the basis of common physical features.

D 20. People who are impulsive
   a. have difficulty separating out a relevant feature from the context in which it is embedded.
   b. can ignore irrelevant perceptual information.
   c. withhold answers until they have carefully evaluated their ideas.
   d. respond to a problem in a quick, cursory, and inaccurate manner.

D 21. The first practical test to measure the mental capabilities of schoolchildren was published by
   a. Jean Piaget.
   b. Lawrence Kohlberg.
   c. David Wechsler.
   d. none of the above.

B 22. Which of the following statements is *not* true?
   a. Children who score high on IQ tests also do well in school.
   b. IQ tests emphasize the child's ability to learn new ideas rather than what he or she has already learned.
   c. IQ scores for the same person can differ at different stages of development.
   d. IQ scores can be used to identify slow learners and gifted children.

C 23. Which of the following terms refers to motor difficulties, poor coordination, and awkwardness?
   a. dyslexia
   b. dysgraphia
   c. dyskinesia
   d. aphasia

D 24. Learning disabilities result from
   a. mental deficiency.
   b. sensory handicaps.
   c. behavioral disturbances.
   d. none of the above.

C 25. Which of the following statements is *not* true?
   a. Children with learning disabilities may experience loss of self-esteem.
   b. The difficulties observed in learning-disabled school-age children are typical of preschool children.
   c. Learning disabilities tend to increase with age.
   d. There is little evidence that learning disabilities are produced by slight abnormalities in brain development.

Matching

A. Kohlberg's levels of morality:

_C_ 1. Obedience and punishment orientation
_E_ 2. Instrumental exchange orientation
_B_ 3. Good boy/nice girl orientation
_F_ 4. Law and order morality
_A_ 5. Social contract orientation
_D_ 6. Universal ethical principles orientation

a. Sees rules and laws in relation to the group that makes them.
b. Conforms to rules to gain approval.
c. Obeys rules set by authority to avoid punishment.
d. Follows self-chosen universal principles.
e. Follows rules to get rewards or return a fair exchange.
f. Conforms blindly to rules or laws for the good of society.

B. Cognitive styles:

_A_ 1. Field independent
_B_ 2. Impulsive
_C_ 3. Field dependent
_D_ 4. Reflective

a. Can ignore irrelevant perceptual information.
b. Responds too quickly and frequently makes errors.
c. Cannot consider objects separately from their context.
d. Slow and deliberate in making decisions.

C. Learning disabilities:

_B_ 1. Dysgraphia
_A_ 2. Dyslexia
_E_ 3. Dyscalcula
_C_ 4. Dyskinesia
_D_ 5. Aphasia

a. Inability to read or spell.
b. Difficulty in writing.
c. Poor coordination, awkwardness.
d. Inability to speak or comprehend what is said.
e. Inability to manipulate numbers.

ANSWERS

True or False

1. F
2. T
3. T
4. F
5. F
6. T
7. F
8. T
9. T
10. F
11. F
12. F
13. T
14. T
15. F
16. T
17. F
18. F
19. T
20. F

21. T
22. T
23. F
24. F
25. T

Sentence Completion

1. middle childhood
2. myelinization
3. physical fitness
4. concrete operations
5. conservation
6. intension, extension
7. figuring it out
8. social-relational
9. moral reasoning
10. autonomous morality
11. reasoning behind the answers
12. preconventional
13. male
14. clear, direct
15. selective
16. chunking, clustering
17. impulsive
18. Alfred Binet
19. standardized group performance
20. verbal, logical
21. school achievement
22. dysgraphia
23. behavior
24. developmental
25. frustration, self-esteem

Multiple Choice

1. a
2. a
3. d
4. b
5. b
6. c
7. c
8. d
9. b
10. a
11. c
12. c
13. b

14. d
15. c
16. a
17. d
18. a
19. b
20. d
21. d
22. b
23. c
24. d
25. c

Matching

A. 1. c
   2. e
   3. b
   4. f
   5. a
   6. d

B. 1. a
   2. b
   3. c
   4. d

C. 1. b
   2. a
   3. e
   4. c
   5. d

Chapter 8

MIDDLE CHILDHOOD:
PERSONALITY AND SOCIAL DEVELOPMENT

CHAPTER OUTLINE

Personality
    Freud's Latency Stage
    Erikson's Stage of Industry vs. Inferiority
    Development of Self
        Changes in Self-Awareness
        Self-Esteem
        Parental Influence on Self-Esteem
Socialization in Middle Childhood
    The Impact of Siblings
        Sibling Status: Birth Order
        Sibling Interactions
    Peer Interactions
        Characteristics
        Functions of the Peer Group
        Peer Status
        Social Competencies and Peers
        Development of Children's Friendships
    The Impact of Television
        Cognitive and Affective Development
        Violence and Aggression
Problems in Adjustment
    Sources of Stress
    Resilient Children
    Fear of AIDS in School
    Adjustment Reactions of Children
        Aggression
        Fear and Anxiety
        Childhood Depression

SUMMARY OF KEY CONCEPTS

1. The child's personality is influenced by many experiences during middle childhood. During this period the evaluations of significant others become part of the child's view of self.

2. According to Erikson, during the school years children must resolve the crisis of industry versus inferiority. In doing so they form an attitude about their ability to work and be productive.

3. *Self-concept* includes the child's physical appearance (including gender and activities), psychological experience (including feelings), and social sense of self. Children's *self-esteem* is influenced by their successes and accomplishments and by the amount of firm, affectionate direction they receive from their parents.

4. Siblings play an important role in a child's development. They serve as models of behavior, sources of comfort, and competitors for parental attention. Sibling interactions provide a way for children to learn how to get along with others.

5. The order in which children are born can affect their achievement and social interactions. Only children do not have to learn to cooperate or share resources with other children.

6. Peer interactions become more frequent during the school years. Peer groups serve several functions, including providing social approval, companionship, and a source of knowledge. *Peer status* refers to the degree to which a child is accepted by others. Factors in acceptance are friendliness, prosocial behavior, attractiveness, and social competence.

7. Children's understanding of friendship changes during childhood. According to Selman, children's ability to make and sustain friendships develops in five distinct stages.

8. Television is a significant and pervasive socializing agent that influences children's aggressive behavior, social attitudes and behavior, and general knowledge.

9. Children's reactions to stress depend on the amount of family and social support provided to them, their ability to understand events, and their own personal strengths. Fear of AIDS has created additional problems for children infected with the disease.

10. Some children have difficulty making the many adjustments required by school and family circumstances. Such children are especially prone to aggressive behaviors, anxiety and fears, and childhood depression.

KEY TERMS AND PHRASES

self-concept
self-esteem
body esteem
birth order
sociometry
sociogram
time out

REVIEW QUESTIONS

1. How do Freud and Erikson view the development of the personality during middle childhood?

2. What is meant by self-concept? How does it change during middle childhood?

3. Briefly describe the impact of birth order and sibling interactions on development in middle childhood.

4. What are the functions of the peer group?

5. What factors account for the differences in social status among schoolchildren?

6. List the five stages in the development of children's friendships.

7. What effect, if any, does television have on the cognitive and affective development of children?

8. What are the most common sources of stress among elementary school children?

9. Briefly describe the most common adjustment reactions of children under stress.

EXERCISES

1. Create a sociogram illustrating the patterns of attraction and dislike among the members of a peer group you are familiar with.

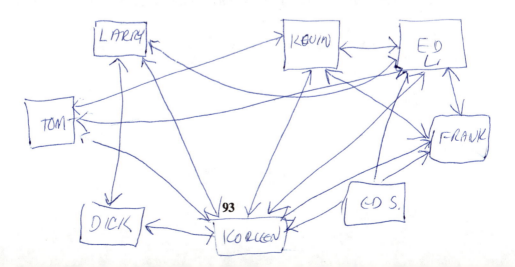

2. Complete the following chart on Selman's stages in the development of friendships.

STAGE	NAME OF STAGE	AGE RANGE	EXPLANATION
1			
2			
3			
4			
5			

QUIZ

True or False

_F_ 1. The impact of friends, relatives, and teachers becomes less significant during the school years.

_T_ 2. Erikson's fourth stage of psychosocial development is the stage of industry versus inferiority.

_F_ 3. Self-esteem refers to the person's sense of his or her own identity.

_T_ 4. Children use gender, age, size, and appearance in defining the self.

_T_ 5. According to Selman, an introspective self emerges at the age of 8.

_F_ 6. Children with low self-esteem are more independent than children with high self-esteem.

_T_ 7. Children with high self-esteem have parents who enforce rules in a firm and decisive manner.

_F_ 8. The more children there are in a family, the more intense and powerful their sibling relations are.

_F_ 9. Only children are more likely to be competitive rather than cooperative in games.

_F_ 10. Sibling interactions do not differ significantly from peer interactions.

_T_ 11. One function of peer groups is to provide a testing ground for new behavior.

_T_ 12. The technique known as sociometry is used to study social relations among peers.

_F_ 13. Children who are academic achievers are likely to be unpopular with their peers.

_T_ 14. Popular children seem to acquire their status by displaying social competence.

_F_ 15. According to Selman, the first stage in the development of children's friendships is fair-weather cooperation.

_T_ 16. The average 2-year-old spends more than two hours a day watching television.

_F_ 17. Researchers have found little correlation between TV watching and children's behavior.

_F_ 18. Children begin to distinguish between fantasy and reality around the age of 3.

_T_ 19. About one-third of children between the ages of 6 and 12 have some form of emotional problem.

_T_ 20. A frequent source of stress for schoolchildren is maternal employment.

_F_ 21. Children raised in stressful family and social environments are unable to develop normally.

_T_ 22. There is no known cure for AIDS.

_F_ 23. Children with learning disabilities behave less aggressively than normal children.

_F_ 24. Anxiety is a rational response to a specific danger.

_T_ 25. Young children who are depressed may stop growing.

Sentence Completion

1. According to Freud, between the ages of 6 to 12 strong sexual feelings are dormant or _LATENT_

2. _SELF CONCEPT_ refers to a person's sense of his or her own identity.

3. In early childhood the self is regarded in _PHYSICAL_ terms.

95

4. Children's use of _SOCIAL COMPARISON_ of competence to define themselves increases dramatically after the age of 7.

5. _SELF-ESTEEM_ is an affective evaluation of one's self, generally assessed in terms of positive or negative traits.

6. _BODY ESTEEM_ refers to a person's evaluation of his or her body.

7. Parents who have _DEFINITE_ values are more likely to rear children who value themselves highly.

8. More than _80_ percent of American children have one or more brothers or sisters.

9. _LATER BORN_ siblings acquire more social skills in negotiating with and accommodating others.

10. Children generally behave in a more _NEGATIVE_ manner toward each other than parents do toward children.

11. Older siblings often function as _TEACHERS_ for young siblings.

12. During middle childhood children interact primarily with others of their own _GENDER_ and _RACE_.

13. _PEER STATUS_ is the degree to which a child is liked and accepted by his or her peers.

14. On the basis of a sociogram, researchers can identify three categories of children: _STARS_, _ISOLATES_ and _REJECTS_.

15. Popular children are physically more _ATTRACTIVE_ than unpopular children.

16. The three dimensions of socially competent performance are _RELEVANCE_, _RESPONSIVENESS_ and _UNDERSTANDING OF RELATIONSHIPS_.

17. In the final stage in the development of friendship, friendships are characterized by their _AUTONOMOUS_ quality. _& INTERDEPENDENT_

18. By the time children graduate from high school they have spent an average of _15,000_ hours in front of the television set.

19. Research on the effects of television on development suggests that it _DOES_ (does/does not) influence behavior.

20. _AGGRESSIVE_ behaviors become more apparent when the child goes to school.

21. Children living in families in which one or both parents suffer from psychiatric disorders are more vulnerable to _EMOTIONAL DISORDERS_

22. Among the factors that distinguish resilient children from vulnerable children are the availability of *social* and the ability to _____ and _*cope*_ the situation at hand. *support*   *understand*

23. The U.S. Public Health Service recommends that children infected with AIDS *should* (should/should not) be allowed to attend school.

24. *Aggression*, like many other behaviors, is maintained by the consequences it elicits.

25. The term *childhood stress* is used to describe children's reactions to a variety of situational and developmental changes in their lives.

Multiple Choice

D 1. In Freud's theory of psychosexual development, the period between the ages of 6 and 12 is the
   a. oral stage.
   b. anal stage.
   c. genital stage.
   d. latency stage.

B 2. The period from 6 to 12 years of age corresponds to Erikson's fourth stage of psychosocial development, the stage of
   a. trust versus mistrust.
   b. industry versus inferiority.
   c. initiative versus guilt.
   d. identity versus role confusion.

A 3. A person's awareness of his or her own abilities and traits is known as
   a. self-concept.
   b. self-esteem.
   c. the introspective self.
   d. the second-person perspective.

A 4. Young children tend to view the self in terms of
   a. physical characteristics.
   b. inner thoughts and feelings.
   c. athletic ability.
   d. social competence.

C 5. According to Selman, children become aware of the distinction between actions and intentions around the age of
   a. 2.
   b. 4.
   c. 6.
   d. 8.

_D_ 6. Which of the following statements is _not_ true?
   a. Children's self-esteem is relatively stable throughout childhood.
   b. Children with high self-esteem are more independent and creative than children with low self-esteem.
   c. Children with high self-esteem will express their views even when they anticipate criticism.
   d. Self-esteem generally becomes less positive during adolescence.

_A_ 7. Parents of children with high self-esteem tend to
   a. set clear limits on behavior.
   b. use physical punishment.
   c. discipline their children through withdrawal of affection.
   d. none of the above.

_B_ 8. Compared to later-born children, firstborn children are more
   a. liberal.
   b. dependent on others' approval.
   c. skilled at negotiating with others.
   d. compliant.

_C_ 9. Research on only children has found that such children
   a. tend to be competitive rather than cooperative.
   b. have many friends.
   c. are less likely to seek the company of their peers.
   d. none of the above.

_D_ 10. Which of the following statements is _not_ true?
   a. Older siblings lack the cognitive maturity to function as substitute parents.
   b. Younger siblings are often disruptive when under the care of older siblings.
   c. Children see themselves as competing for their parents' attention and praise.
   d. Older siblings do not function well as teachers for young siblings.

_C_ 11. Which of the following statements is true?
   a. Peer interactions do not differ significantly from adult-child inter-actions.
   b. Children seek out other children for protection or instruction.
   c. For the most part children choose their own friends.
   d. All of the above.

_D_ 12. Which of the following is a function of peer groups?
   a. provide companionship
   b. provide a testing ground for new behavior
   c. pass on knowledge
   d. all of the above

_B_ 13. Which of the following is *not* a function of peer groups?
   a.   enforcing codes of conduct
   b.   taking care of younger siblings
   c.   reinforcing gender-role behaviors
   d.   All of the above are functions of peer groups.

_B_ 14. The degree to which a child is liked and accepted by his or her peers is termed
   a.   sociometry.
   b.   peer status.
   c.   body esteem.
   d.   social competence.

_C_ 15. In a sociogram, a child who is neither positively nor negatively regarded by peers is known as a (an)
   a.   star.
   b.   reject.
   c.   isolate.
   d.   controversial child.

_A_ 16. Which of the following statements is *not* true?
   a.   Popular children tend to have uncommon first names.
   b.   Popular children are physically more attractive than unpopular children.
   c.   Unpopular children are more likely to act aggressively than popular children.
   d.   Unpopular children tend to play with younger children.

_B_ 17. According to Asher, the three dimensions of social competence are
   a.   attractiveness, responsiveness, and relevance.
   b.   relevance, responsiveness, and understanding of relationships.
   c.   attractiveness, responsiveness, and understanding of relationships.
   d.   intelligence, responsiveness, and relevance.

_C_ 18. According to Selman, before children form friendships they engage in relationships that he terms
   a.   one-way assistance.
   b.   fair-weather cooperation.
   c.   momentary playmateship.
   d.   autonomous relationships.

_A_ 19. According to Selman, the highest stage in the development of friendships is
   a.   autonomous, interdependent relationships.
   b.   intimate and mutually shared relationships.
   c.   fair-weather cooperation.
   d.   one-way assistance.

D 20. Compared to time spent in direct classroom instruction, how much time do children spend watching television?
   a.   considerably more
   b.   much less
   c.   somewhat less
   d.   about the same amount

D 21. Research on the effects of television viewing suggests that it influences children's
   a.   learning.
   b.   behavior.
   c.   neither a nor b.
   d.   both a and b.

B 22. What percentage of school-age children require professional help to cope with problems of adjustment?
   a.   3 percent
   b.   10 percent
   c.   25 percent
   d.   33 percent

A 23. Which of the following statements is *not* true?
   a.   Children of emotionally disturbed parents are less likely to have psychiatric problems themselves.
   b.   Some children appear to be invulnerable to the effects of stressful experiences.
   c.   Social support from a caring adult helps offset the negative effects of stress.
   d.   Resilient children are friendly and independent.

C 24. The best treatment for aggressive behavior is
   a.   physical punishment.
   b.   removal of television privileges.
   c.   withdrawal of attention.
   d.   scolding.

B 25. Childhood depression appears to be caused by
   a.   real or imagined danger.
   b.   a sense of loss.
   c.   physiological conditions.
   d.   observation of depressed adults.

Matching

A. Levels of self-awareness in children:

B 1. Physicalistic conception of self

C 2. Awareness of distinction between actions and intentions

A 3. Emergence of introspective self and second-person perspective

a. Children learn to manipulate their inner states and external appearance.
b. Children view "self" only in physical terms.
c. Children believe that psychological and physical experiences are different but consistent.

B. Peer status categories:

C 1. Stars
D 2. Isolates

A 3. Rejects
B 4. Controversial children

a. Children who are actively disliked.
b. Children who are strongly liked by some peers and strongly disliked by others.
c. Children who are actively liked.
d. Children who are neither actively liked nor actively disliked.

C. Stages in the development of friendship:

C 0. Momentary playmateship

D 1. One-way assistance

A 2. Fair-weather cooperation

E 3. Intimate, mutually shared relationship
B 4. Autonomous, interdependent relationship

a. Children become aware of the reciprocal nature of friendships
b. Friends rely on each other for emotional support but are not possessive
c. Friends are valued for toys, physical attributes, and proximity.
d. The friend performs activities that the child wants accomplished.
e. Friendships are a means to develop mutual intimacy and support.

ANSWERS

True or False

1. F
2. T
3. F
4. T
5. T

6. F
7. T
8. F
9. F
10. F
11. T
12. T
13. F
14. T

15. F
16. T
17. F
18. F
19. T
20. T
21. F
22. T
23. F
24. F
25. T

Sentence Completion

1. latent
2. self-concept
3. physical
4. social comparison
5. self-esteem
6. body esteem
7. definite
8. 80
9. later-born
10. negative
11. teachers
12. gender, race
13. peer status
14. stars, isolates, rejects
15. attractive
16. relevance, responsiveness, understanding of relationships
17. autonomous, interdependent
18. 15,000
19. does
20. aggressive
21. emotional disorders
22. social support, understand, cope with
23. should
24. aggression
25. childhood stress

Multiple Choice

1. d
2. b
3. a
4. a
5. c
6. d
7. a
8. b
9. c
10. d
11. c
12. d
13. b
14. b
15. c
16. a
17. b
18. c
19. a
20. d
21. d
22. b
23. a
24. c
25. b

Matching

A. 1. b
   2. c
   3. a

B. 1. c
   2. d
   3. a
   4. b

C. 0. c
   1. d
   2. a
   3. e
   4. b

Chapter 9

ADOLESCENCE:
PHYSICAL, COGNITIVE, AND MORAL DEVELOPMENT

CHAPTER OUTLINE

Physical and Sexual Development
    Physical Growth
    Puberty
        Primary Sex Characteristics
        Secondary Sex Characteristics
    Secular Growth Trends
    Varying Rates of Development
        Early and Late Maturation
        The Impact of Menarche
    Sexual Attitudes and Behavior
        Heterosexual Behavior
        Homosexuality
        Teenage Pregnancy
        Sex Education
Cognitive Development
    Formal Operations (11-15 Years)
        Problem-Solving Skills
        Adolescent Idealism
        Limitations of Piaget's Theory
    Adolescent Egocentrism
    Moral Reasoning
    Value Systems
    Political Awareness

SUMMARY OF KEY CONCEPTS

1. During adolescence a dramatic change in height, weight, and body proportions takes place; this is known as the *adolescent growth spurt*. There are always variations in physical, emotional, and intellectual development among adolescents of the same age.

2. *Puberty* is the period during which an individual reaches sexual maturity. In the prepubescent stage, *secondary sex characteristics* begin to develop. In the pubescent stage, the reproductive organs begin to produce ova or sperm. In the postpubescent stage, the sex organs become fully capable of adult functioning.

3. Today adolescents reach puberty at an earlier age than teenagers born several generations ago. Secular growth trends are believed to be influenced by biological and environmental factors.

4. The physical changes that occur during adolescence have important effects on psychological development, especially in the area of self-concept. Early-maturing boys generally excel at sports, in social activities, and in areas of leadership. The impact of timing of maturation is less clear for girls.

5. Today more teenagers are sexually active and at younger ages than ever before; this is especially true for girls. Two consequences of unprotected sexual behavior are a rising birthrate and an increase in venereal disease among teenagers. Adolescents sometimes experiment with homosexual behavior.

6. Most schools have sex education programs for high-school students. The content of such courses varies considerably and often does not include enough information on how to prevent pregnancy or sexually transmitted disease.

7. According to Piaget, the stage of formal operations emerges between the ages of 11 and 15. During this stage the adolescent becomes able to deal with abstractions and reason deductively.

8. *Adolescent egocentrism* is the tendency of adolescents to become self-absorbed and to have exaggerated notions of self-importance. Two concepts related to adolescent egocentrism are the *imaginary audience* and the *personal fable*.

9. According to Kohlberg, early adolescence is characterized by *conventional morality*, or reasoning based on winning approval and maintaining the status quo. During middle and late adolescence the range of moral judgments broadens as the individual enters the stage of *postconventional morality*, in which reasoning is based on self-accepted principles of ethics and justice.

10. The formation of a value system and political attitudes appears to follow a developmental trend. The influence of parents in these areas seems to have diminished, while the media, peers, and specific political events have emerged as important influences.

KEY TERMS AND PHRASES

puberty — STAGE AT WHICH INDIVIDUAL REACHES SEXUAL MATURITY & CAN REPRODUCE.

adolescent growth spurt — PERIOD OF GROWTH ACCELERATION OCCURING EARLY IN ADOLESCENTS

secondary sex characteristics — PHYSICAL FEATURES, OTHER THAN GENITALS, THAT DISTINGUISH WOMEN FROM MEN.

menarche — FIRST OCCURRENCE OF MENSTRUATION

adolescent egocentrism — TENDENCY OF ADOLESCENTS TO BELIEVE THAT OTHER PEOPLE ARE PREOCCUPIED WITH THEM.

imaginary audience — BELIEF THAT THEY ARE FOCUS OF OTHER'S ATTENTION.

personal fable

KOHLBERG {
conventional morality — 2ND LEVEL OF MORAL REASONING — DESIRE TO PRESERVE HARMONIOUS INTERPERSONAL RELATIONSHIPS & TO OBEY EXISTING FORMAL RULES, LAWS & SOCIETAL STDS.

postconventional morality — 3RD LEVEL OF MORAL REASONING — MORALITY BASED ON APPEALS TO SOCIAL AGREEMENTS & DEMOCRATIC PRINCIPLES, & THE BASIC PRINCIPLES OF ETHICS & HUMAN RIGHTS.
}

REVIEW QUESTIONS

1. Briefly describe the changes that occur as part of the adolescent growth spurt.

2. What are the three stages of puberty? What changes occur in each stage?

3. What effects do early and late maturation have on adolescent boys and girls?

4. How have sexual attitudes and behavior among adolescents changed in recent generations?

5. How widespread is teenage pregnancy? What are the risks associated with such pregnancies?

6. What is meant by formal-operational thought?

7. Briefly describe adolescent egocentrism and the related concepts of the imaginary audience and the personal fable.

8. What changes in moral reasoning occur during adolescence, according to Kohlberg?

9. Briefly describe the development of value systems and political awareness in adolescents.

EXERCISES

1. Complete the chart by describing the physical changes that occur in each stage of puberty.

STAGE	MALES	FEMALES
Prepubescent		
Pubescent		
Postpubescent		

2. Describe the various aspects of adolescent egocentrism.

ASPECT	DESCRIPTION
Adolescent egocentrism	
Abiding self	
Transient self	
Imaginary audience	
Personal fable	

QUIZ

<u>True or False</u>

_T_ 1. The first physical changes that occur during adolescence occur in the body's hormonal makeup.

_F_ 2. The adolescent growth spurt generally begins about two years later in girls than in boys.

_T_ 3. By age 17 girls may have two-and-a-half times as much body fat as boys.

_F_ 4. Primary sex characteristics are nongenital physical features that distinguish the sexes.

_F_ 5. Secondary sex characteristics begin to develop during the postpubescent stage of puberty.

_T_ 6. The first indication of approaching sexual maturity in a girl is budding of the breasts.

_T_ 7. Secular growth trends refer to variations in human physical growth found throughout the world.

F 8. Research has shown that girls who mature early have a distinct advantage over those who mature late.

F 9. For most girls menarche is a traumatic experience.

T 10. In late adolescence sexual relationships tend to be based on mutuality.

F 11. Studies of adolescent sexuality indicate that homosexual experiences become increasingly frequent after the age of 15.

T 12. Rates of teenage pregnancy are higher in the United States than in any other industrialized nation.

F 13. Few adolescent fathers are interested in caring for their children.

T 14. Sexually active teenagers who have taken sex education courses are less likely to become pregnant.

F 15. According to Piaget, the stage of formal operations is reached at about age 16.

F 16. Adolescents are not yet able to extrapolate beyond directly observable results.

F 17. The tendency of adolescents to believe that other people are as preoccupied with their behavior and appearance as they themselves are is known as adolescent idealism.

T 18. Adolescents continually create an imaginary audience before whom they perform.

T 19. In early adolescence people shift to the level of moral reasoning known as conventional morality.

F 20. In the postconventional stage of moral development, the person is concerned with maintaining good relations with others and winning their approval.

T 21. Not all people reach the highest stage of postconventional morality.

T 22. Adolescents tend to be attracted to rigid, authoritarian ideologies.

F 23. Because adolescents like to challenge ideologies, they often become actively involved in political movements.

T 24. According to Keniston, political issues serve as catalysts for moral development.

T 25. The majority of high school seniors do not understand the American political system.

Sentence Completion

1. *PUBERTY* is the period of adolescence during which an individual reaches sexual maturity.

2. The period of accelerated growth known as the *ADOLESCENT GROWTH SPURT* usually lasts from two to three years.

3. Total body weight less total body fat yields *LEAN BODY MASS*.

4. Changes in voice and body hair in adolescents are examples of the development of *SECONDARY SEX CHARACTERISTICS*.

5. A girl's first menstruation is known as *MENARCHE*.

6. The deepening of the voice of an adolescent male is caused by an enlargement of the *LARYNX* and lengthening of the *VOCAL CHORDS*.

7. Children in different parts of the world seem to be reaching puberty *EARLIER* than their parents did.

8. Early maturation is *LESS* advantageous for girls than it is for boys.

9. Young adolescents who have more *KNOWLEDGE* about menarche before experiencing it are more likely to have positive reactions to it.

10. According to Siegel, changes in adolescent sexual behavior should be characterized as *EVOLUTIONARY* rather than *REVOLUTIONARY*.

11. In a recent study, *15* percent of boys and *10* percent of girls reported having had a homosexual experience.

12. Babies of teenage mothers have twice the normal chance of being born *PREMATURELY* or with *LOW BIRTH WEIGHT*, *NEUROLOGICAL DEFECTS OR BIRTH INJURIES*.

13. Sex education classes *DO NOT* (do/do not) influence an adolescent's choice to have or not have sex.

14. In the stage of formal operations individuals become able to consider *ABSTRACT* concepts.

15. The adolescent's increased freedom in forming hypotheses often creates problems in making *DECISIONS*.

16. Interest in theoretical ideas leads adolescents to construct *IDEAL* families, societies, and religions.

17. According to Elkind, in searching to know who they are adolescents become *SELF-ABSORBED*.

18. The characteristics of the self that are assumed to be relatively stable or unchanging are termed the _An____ *HOLDING SELF*; those that are assumed to be temporary are termed the _TRANSIENT SELF_.

19. Many adolescents develop a _PERSONAL FABLE_, an ongoing, private, and imaginary story in which they play the leading role.

20. Moral judgments at the _PRE-CONVENTIONAL_ level are based on the anticipated outcomes of a behavior--punishment and reward.

21. At the _POST CONVENTIONAL_ level of morality the individual defines moral values and principles apart from the authority of groups or persons.

22. The level at which a person reasons about moral issues may vary from one _SITUATION_ to another.

23. During adolescents children consider various _IDEOLOGIES_ to provide them with answers to philosophical questions.

24. Younger adolescents tend to _PERSONALIZE_ political issues, whereas older adolescents tend to evaluate their effects on _SOCIETY AS A WHOLE_.

25. The political socialization that takes place in the school is aimed at reinforcing the concept of _OBEDIENCE TO AUTHORITY_

Multiple Choice

____1.	The period of adolescence during which an individual reaches sexual maturity is known as
	a.	menarche.
	(b.)	puberty.
	c.	the adolescent growth spurt.
	d.	the stage of secular growth.

____2.	In girls, the adolescent growth spurt usually begins between the ages of
	(a.)	9 and 11.
	b.	12 and 14.
	c.	15 and 18.
	d.	none of the above.

____3. One of the earliest changes in both sexes is
	a.	growth in lean body mass.
	b.	production of ova or sperm.
	(c.)	the addition of subcutaneous fat.
	d.	the appearance of facial hair.

_____4. Breasts, body hair, and voice change are examples of
   a. primary sex characteristics.
   b. secondary sex characteristics.
   c. tertiary sex characteristics.
   d. none of the above.

_____5. Production of ova or sperm begins during the
   a. semipubescent stage.
   b. prepubescent stage.
   c. pubescent stage.
   d. postpubescent stage.

_____6. Which of the following statements is true?
   a. Children in different parts of the world are reaching puberty earlier than their parents did.
   b. A young woman will probably be almost an inch taller than her mother.
   c. Today's adolescents reach full adult height earlier than their ancestors did.
   d. All of the above.

_____7. Boys who mature early
   a. tend to excel at sports.
   b. are less popular than their peers.
   c. are likely to avoid extracurricular activities.
   d. are rebuffed by early-maturing girls.

_____8. Early-maturing girls are more likely than late-maturing girls to
   a. perform well academically.
   b. have behavior problems.
   c. be satisfied with their bodies.
   d. be dependent and lack social graces.

_____9. Which of the following statements is *not* true?
   a. Changes in adolescent sexual behavior are best described as evolutionary.
   b. The vast majority of adolescents approve of premarital sexual intercourse.
   c. The greatest changes in adolescent sexual behavior have occurred among boys.
   d. Teenagers are initiating sexual activity at increasingly younger ages.

_____10. According to Kinsey and his colleagues, what proportion of American males have had some homosexual experience?
   a. 5 percent
   b. 12 percent
   c. 18 percent
   d. 37 percent

_____11. Which of the following statements is *not* true?
    a. Only Sweden and France have higher rates of teenage pregnancy than the United States.
    b. nearly 40 percent of teenage pregnancies in the United States are terminated by abortion.
    c. Once a teenager gets pregnant for the first time, the odds are that she will do so again within three years.
    d. The younger the mother, the greater the risk that her baby will die in infancy.

_____12. Adolescent fathers
    a. are difficult to identify.
    b. are concerned about their newborn children.
    c. are interested in caring for their children.
    d. all of the above.

_____13. Which of the following statements is true?
    a. Few states have mandated sex education classes.
    b. Sex education classes are an important factor in an adolescent's choice to have or not have sex.
    c. Sexually active girls who have taken sex education courses are less likely to become pregnant.
    d. All of the above.

_____14. According to Piaget, between the ages of 11 and 15 the child enters which stage of cognitive development?
    a. the sensorimotor stage
    b. the preoperational stage
    c. the concrete-operational stage
    d. none of the above

_____15. Which of the following is a cognitive competence that is generally acquired during adolescence?
    a. making careful, objective observations
    b. developing hypotheses
    c. solving problems through trial and error
    d. all of the above

_____16. Adolescent egocentrism refers to
    a. the belief that other people are preoccupied with one's behavior and appearance.
    b. inability to distinguish reality from one's own point of view.
    c. willingness to reveal to others characteristics of the self that are assumed to be unchanging.
    d. efforts to construct ideal families, societies, and religions.

____17. An adolescent's ongoing, private, and imaginary story is referred to as his or her
  a. imaginary audience.
  b. abiding self.
  c. transient self.
  d. personal fable.

____18. In which stage of moral development are right and wrong evaluated in terms of conformity to societal rules and regulations?
  a. unconventional
  b. preconventional
  c. conventional
  d. postconventional

____19. The majority of adolescents and adults typically reason at which level of morality?
  a. unconventional
  b. preconventional
  c. conventional
  d. postconventional

____20. Which of the following statements is *not* true?
  a. At the postconventional level of morality, people control their moral decisions internally.
  b. Once they reach the postconventional level, people consistently reason at that level.
  c. People's behavior may not always coincide with their moral judgments.
  d. Moral development is typically upward, gradual, and in a stagelike sequence.

____21. In developing a personal philosophy, adolescents tend to seek guidance from
  a. their parents' value systems.
  b. the beliefs of teachers and guidance counselors.
  c. ideological doctrines.
  d. teen magazines.

____22. Which of the following is an important influence on adolescents' value systems?
  a. historical events
  b. cultural emphases
  c. personal experiences
  d. all of the above

_____23. Which of the following statements is *not* true?
- (a.) Adolescents are especially likely to become actively involved in political movements.
- b. Adolescents tend to be intolerant of civil liberties.
- c. Younger adolescents tend to personalize issues of political philosophy.
- d. According to Keniston, political issues may serve as catalysts for moral development.

_____24. The political socialization that takes place in schools is designed to reinforce the concept of
- a. freedom of religion.
- (b.) obedience to authority.
- c. the social contract.
- d. universal ethical principles.

_____25. Which of the following statements is true?
- (a.) The influence of the family on children's political development has diminished.
- b. The political attitudes of children are quite different from those of their parents.
- c. Mothers have become more important than fathers in transmitting political attitudes.
- d. The school has become the most significant agent of political socialization.

Matching

A. Stages of puberty:

_C_1. Prepubescent

_B_2. Pubescent

_A_3. Postpubescent

- a. Sex organs are capable of adult functioning.
- b. Ova or sperm production begins.
- c. The secondary sex characteristics begin to develop.

B. Stages of moral reasoning:

_B_1. Stage 3 (conventional)

_D_2. Stage 4 (conventional)

_A_3. Stage 5 (postconventional)

_C_4. Stage 6 (postconventional)

- a. Moral action is judged in terms of individual rights.
- b. The person is concerned with maintaining good relations with others.
- c. Right is defined by the individual's conscience.
- d. Right and wrong are evaluated in terms of conformity to societal rules.

ANSWERS

True or False

1. T
2. F
3. T
4. F
5. F
6. T
7. T
8. F
9. F
10. T
11. F
12. T
13. F
14. T
15. F
16. F
17. F
18. T
19. T
20. F
21. T
22. T
23. F
24. T
25. T

Sentence Completion

1. puberty
2. adolescent growth spurt
3. lean body mass
4. secondary sex characteristics
5. menarche
6. larynx, vocal cords
7. earlier
8. less
9. knowledge
10. evolutionary, revolutionary
11. 15, 10
12. prematurely, low birthweight, neurological defects, birth injuries
13. do not
14. abstract
15. decisions
16. ideal
17. self-absorbed
18. abiding self, transient self
19. personal fable
20. preconventional
21. postconventional
22. situation
23. ideologies
24. personalize, society as a whole
25. obedience to authority

Multiple Choice

1. b
2. a
3. c
4. b
5. c
6. d
7. a
8. b
9. c
10. d
11. a
12. d
13. c
14. d
15. b
16. a
17. d
18. c
19. c
20. b
21. c
22. d
23. a
24. b
25. a

Matching

A. 1. c
   2. b
   3. a

B. 1. b
   2. d
   3. a
   4. c

Chapter 10

ADOLESCENCE:
PERSONALITY AND SOCIAL DEVELOPMENT

CHAPTER OUTLINE

Adolescent Identity
    Ethnic and Racial Identity
    Searching for Origins: Adopted Adolescents
    Adolescent Turmoil: Fact or Fiction?
Adolescents and Their Parents
    Parent-Adolescent Conflict
    Establishing Independence and Autonomy
Adolescent Peer Relations
    The Society of Adolescents
        Peer-Group Composition
        Adolescent Friendships
        Conformity
Vocational Choice
    Choosing a Career
    Adolescent Employment
Problem Behavior
    Depression
    Adolescent Suicide
        Danger Signs of Adolescent Suicide
    Eating Disturbances
    Conduct Disorders
    Substance Abuse
        Alcohol
        Marijuana

SUMMARY OF KEY CONCEPTS

1. Adolescence is the period in which the individual establishes an integrated identity. An important aspect of identity for adolescents of ethnic or racial origins.

2. Although many adolescents experience emotional upheaval over identity, parent and peer relations, and other issues, others pass through this period with considerably less stress and strain. Adopted adolescents may have more difficulty establishing their identity.

3. The majority of teenagers get along with their parents. The conflicts that do occur concern independence, sexuality, and choices in hair and dress styles. Parents who are overly controlling are more likely to have conflicts with their adolescent children.

4. To establish their own identity, adolescents must become independent of their families. They must find other ways to meet their material and emotional needs and make their own decisions about their behavior and values.

5. The peer group is an important agent of socialization during adolescence. Its standards and values often conflict with those of the family.

6. Intimate friendships begin to emerge in adolescence and help the individual cope with the stresses associated with this period. The pursuit of popularity often leads adolescents to conform to group pressures.

7. For young people the choice of a vocation is often difficult. Gender stereo-typing imposes vocational limitations on women and deprives them of much encouragement.

8. Adolescents who work gain useful social and work skills. However, youth employment may have negative consequences for some adolescents.

9. Adolescents are prone to many of the same social and psychological problems that are experienced by adults, including depression, eating disorders, conduct disorders, and substance abuse. The two most frequently abused drugs among teenagers are alcohol and marijuana.

KEY TERMS AND PHRASES

ego identity
ego continuity
genealogical bewilderment
clique
crowd
mutual role taking
body concept
anorexia nervosa
conduct disorders
unsocialized delinquents
socialized delinquents

FORM OF PSYCHOPATHOLOGY IN WHICH THE INDIVIDUAL CONSISTENTLY VIOLATES THE BASIC RIGHTS OF OTHERS AND/OR NORMS OF SOCIETY.

→ FORM OF CONDUCT DISORDER IN WHICH THE PERSON TYPICALLY FAILS TO DEVELOP A NORMAL DEGREE OF EMPATHY, AFFECTION & ATTACHMENT TO OTHERS. USUALLY ASSOCIATED W. HOMES CHARACTERIZED BY PARENTAL REJECTION & HARD DISCIPLINE.

REVIEW QUESTIONS

1. According to Erikson, what is the major task of the individual during adolescence?

2. What are some of the problems encountered by adolescents in attempting to develop a sense of their own identity?

3. To what extent do parents influence their adolescent children? In what areas do parents and adolescents come into conflict?

4. Briefly describe the society of adolescents.

5. Why is choosing a career a long and complex process? What special problems are encountered by young women in making career decisions?

6. Briefly describe some positive and negative aspects of adolescent employment.

7. What kinds of problem behavior occur among adolescents?

8. What are some early warning signs of suicide among adolescents?

9. What is meant by body concept? What is anorexia nervosa?

10. Distinguish between unsocialized and socialized delinquents.

EXERCISES

1. Describe the stages in career decision making.

AGE	DESCRIPTION
5-10	
10-15	

15-25

_____

25-40

_____

2. List as many early-warning signs of suicide among adolescents as you can think of.

QUIZ

<u>True or False</u>

_T_ 1. During the early years of adolescence there is a decrease in self-awareness.

_F_ 2. The establishment of one's identity is usually complete by the age of 15.

_T_ 3. The self-concept of black adolescents is as positive as that of white adolescents.

_F_ 4. Adoptive parents are generally informed about their child's family history.

_T_ 5. Adopted adolescents who do not know their family history may experience a feeling of incompleteness known as genealogical bereavement.

_F_ 6. Recent research has confirmed that the majority of adolescents experience emotional turmoil.

_T_ 7. Adolescents tend to adopt their parents' views on social, moral, and political issues.

_F_ 8. Conflicts between adolescents and their parents are more frequent when the parents are authoritative.

_F_ 9. Most adolescents become independent from their parents at around age 18.

_T_ 10. Most observers agree that there is an "adolescent society."

_T_ 11. Adolescents spend more time talking to peers than in any other activity.

_F_ 12. A same-gender group of adolescents is known as a crowd.

_T_ 13. Adolescent intimacy is related to the ability to engage in mutual role taking.

_T_ 14. Adolescents are less likely to conform to peers than younger children.

_F_ 15. Choosing a career is less difficult today than it was in the past.

_F_ 16. Research has shown that early employment is associated with greater social responsibility.

_T_ 17. Adolescent depression is similar to depression in adults.

_F_ 18. Suicide is the most frequent cause of death among 15- to 24-year-olds.

_T_ 19. A major cause of adolescent suicide is excessive pressure to excel.

_T_ 20. The condition known as anorexia nervosa is characterized by voluntary restriction of food intake.

_F_ 21. The majority of conduct disorders involve violent crimes.

_T_ 22. Unsocialized delinquents tend to come from broken homes characterized by high levels of family hostility.

_T_ 23. Most antisocial teenagers do not become antisocial adults.

_F_ 24. The most frequently used drug among teenagers in the United States is cocaine.

_T_ 25. There has been a significant increase in the potency of "street" marijuana in the past decade.

Sentence Completion

1. The sense of urgency experienced by most adolescents reflects the rapid and varied _____ they encounter during this time of life.
   TRANSFORMATIONS

2. The major task of the individual during adolescence is the formation of a secure
   EGO . IDENTITY

3. During the transition from childhood to adolescents most boys and girls trade dependency on their _____ for dependency on their _PEERS_.
   PARENTS

119

4. An important aspect of identity for adolescents is awareness of *ETHNIC* or *RACIAL* origins.

5. The term *GENEALOGICAL BEWILDERMENT* describes the feelings of incompleteness that are often experienced by adolescent adoptees.

6. The concept of adolescence as a time of *STORM* and *STRESS* is built into many theories of development.

7. During the 1960s and early 1970s the term *GENERATION GAP* was coined to refer to the generalized disenchantment of adolescents for their parents' way of life.

8. *AUTHORITATIVE* parents appear to have more effective interactions with their adolescent children than parents who are overly *PERMISSIVE* or *AUTHORITARIAN*

9. According to Steinberg, one factor contributing to parent-adolescent conflict is that teenagers are *PHYSICALLY* ready to leave home before they can be *ECONOMICALLY* independent of their parents.

10. Becoming independent is a *GRADUAL* process.

11. Recent research suggests that the adolescent subculture is not *UNIFIED*.

12. Authority in many adolescent organizations tends to be *LATERAL* rather than *VERTICAL*

13. In the prepubescent period children band together in same-gender groups known as *CLIQUES*

14. Contrary to popular belief, adolescents generally are not *FICKLE* in their social relationships.

15. Adolescents are *LESS* likely to conform to peers than younger children.

16. One of the most difficult and potentially frustrating tasks of adolescence is the choice of a *CAREER*

17. Adolescent employment is associated with greater *PERSONAL* responsibility but not with greater *SOCIAL* responsibility.

18. The chief tool for treating depression in teenagers is *PSYCHOTHERAPY*.

19. The rate of suicide among teenagers has *DOUBLED* since the 1960s.

20. In situations in which an adolescent is in danger of committing suicide, it is important to *STAY WITH* the teenager until the immediate crisis is resolved.

21. Anorexia nervosa is characterized by voluntary restriction of food intake, resulting in chronic *UNDERNUTRITION*, *WEIGHT LOSS*, and occasionally *DEATH*.

22. Adolescent _CONDUCT DISORDERS_ are persistent behaviors that violate the basic rights of others and/or the norms of society.

23. _SOCIALIZED_ delinquents are products of social disadvantage and parental neglect.

24. _ALCOHOL_ is the most frequently used drug among teenagers in the United States.

25. The body's immediate responses to inhaling _MARIJUANA_ include contraction of the pupils, increased heart rate, and decreased reaction time.

Multiple Choice

D 1. Which of the following is _not_ a component of ego identity?
    a.   unity
    b.   continuity
    c.   mutuality
    (d.)   self-diffusion

A 2. Early adolescence is marked by an increase in
    (a.)   self-awareness.
    b.   self-acceptance.
    c.   self-aggrandizement.
    d.   self-effacement.

C 3. The process of establishing one's identity
    a.   is complete by the thirteenth birthday.
    b.   usually occurs between the ages of 13 and 15.
    (c.)   may take up to ten years to complete.
    d.   may be skipped entirely.

B 4. The sense that one's current self-perceptions are connected to those of the past and the future is known as
    a.   genealogical bewilderment.
    (b.)   ego continuity.
    c.   self-diffusion..
    d.   perceptual unity.

D 5. Which of the following statements is _not_ true?
    a.   Symptoms of anxiety were found in 65 percent of a sample of normal adolescents.
    b.   For most adolescents, changes in identity and relations with others are gradual and undramatic.
    c.   A longitudinal study found that adolescents maintained a stable sense of themselves throughout a six-year period.
    (d.)   Most adolescents resent their parents, avoid responsibility, and are socially anxious.

C 6. Adolescents are most likely to differ from their parents on issues related to
   a. politics.
   b. moral values.
   c. matters of personal taste.
   d. social issues.

A 7. Parent-adolescent conflict is least likely when the parents are
   a. authoritative.
   b. permissive.
   c. authoritarian.
   d. uninvolved.

D 8. The term *autonomy* refers to
   a. economic independence.
   b. physical separation.
   c. emotional separation.
   d. all of the above.

B 9. Which of the following statements is *not* true?
   a. Most researchers acknowledge the reality of an adolescent "society."
   b. The adolescent subculture alienates high school students from their parents.
   c. The adolescent subculture is not unified.
   d. The function of the adolescent society is to create a context in which adolescents work out mutual problems.

B 10. In which of the following activities do adolescents spend the most time?
   a. watching television
   b. talking to friends
   c. shopping
   d. studying

C 11. A group of adolescents of both sexes that is held together by its orientation to the future, the social background of its members, and their personality types is a
   a. club.
   b. clique.
   c. crowd.
   d. subculture.

A 12. Adolescent intimacy is related in part to the emerging ability of the individual to engage in
   a. mutual role taking.
   b. hypothetical thought.
   c. gender stereotyping.
   d. moral reasoning.

122

A 13. Conformity to peers reaches a peak in
    a. early to middle childhood.
    b. early adolescence.
    c. late adolescence.
    d. none of the above.

C 14. In the past, vocational choice was dependent on
    a. parental approval.
    b. opinions of peers.
    c. social class.
    d. personal needs.

C 15. At what age does an individual generally gain a worker identity by choosing a vocation and preparing for it?
    a. 5-10
    b. 10-15
    c. 15-25
    d. 25-40

D 16. Which of the following traits is *not* affected by adolescent work experience?
    a. punctuality
    b. dependability
    c. self-reliance
    d. social responsibility

D 17. Which of the following problem behaviors occurs exclusively among adolescents?
    a. drug abuse
    b. depression
    c. obesity
    d. none of the above

B 18. Which of the following is the most effective tool for treating depression in teenagers?
    a. antidepressant drugs
    b. psychotherapy
    c. electroshock treatment
    d. hypnosis

A 19. Which of the following is *not* an early-warning sign of adolescent suicide?
    a. melancholy and feelings of dejection
    b. disturbance in eating habits
    c. preoccupation with death
    d. sudden changes in mood and behavior

B 20. Which of the following is a disorder characterized by episodic, uncontrollable binge eating?
   a.   anorexia nervosa
   (b.) bulimia
   c.   obesity
   d.   all of the above

C 21. What proportion of acts of vandalism, car theft, burglary, and arson are committed by adolescents under the age of 18?
   a.   about 10 percent
   b.   25 percent
   c.   nearly half
   d.   approximately two-thirds

C 22. Which of the following statements is *not* true?
   a.   Unsocialized delinquents tend to come from broken homes characterized by high levels of family hostility.
   b.   Socialized delinquents are able to form close relationships with others.
   c.   Most delinquent teenagers grow up to become antisocial adults.
   d.   Drunkenness and violent crimes become more frequent during the transition from adolescence to young adulthood.

A 23. Researchers have found that almost all high seniors have used
   a.   alcohol.
   b.   marijuana.
   c.   cocaine.
   d.   all of the above.

D 24. Which of the following is *not* a potential side effect of marijuana?
   a.   transitory paranoia
   b.   acute anxiety
   c.   altered awareness of space and time
   d.   increased reaction time

B 25. Which of the following statements is *not* true?
   a.   It is not yet clear what damage long-term use of marijuana may do.
   b.   Materials and concepts are significantly better understood when studied while "high."
   c.   Marijuana use may impair social development by providing a means of artificial relaxation.
   d.   There has been a great increase in the potency of "street" marijuana in the past decade.

Matching

A. Components of ego identity:

_B_ 1. Unity
_A_ 2. Continuity
_C_ 3. Mutuality

    a. Self-definition persists over time.
    b. Self-perceptions are consistent.
    c. Self-perceptions match those held by others.

B. Stages of career development:

_C_ 1. Choosing a vocation and preparing for it.
_A_ 2. Identifying with the worker.
_D_ 3. Becoming productive
_B_ 4. Developing basic working habits

    a. age 5-10
    b. age 10-15
    c. age 15-25
    d. age 25-40

ANSWERS

True or False

1. T
2. F
3. T
4. F
5. T
6. F
7. T
8. F
9. F
10. T
11. T
12. F
13. T
14. T
15. F
16. F
17. T
18. F
19. T
20. T
21. F
22. T
23. T
24. F
25. T

Sentence Completion

1. transformations
2. ego identity
3. parents, peers
4. ethnic, racial
5. genealogical bewilderment
6. storm, stress
7. generation gap
8. authoritative, permissive, authoritarian
9. physically, economically
10. gradual
11. unified
12. lateral, vertical
13. cliques
14. fickle
15. less
16. career
17. personal, social
18. psychotherapy
19. doubled
20. stay with
21. undernutrition, weight loss, death
22. conduct disorders
23. socialized
24. alcohol
25. marijuana

Multiple Choice

1. d
2. a
3. c
4. b
5. d
6. c
7. a
8. d
9. b
10. b
11. c
12. a
13. a
14. c
15. c
16. d
17. d
18. b
19. a
20. b
21. c
22. c
23. a
24. d
25. b

Matching

A. 1. b
   2. a
   3. c

B. 1. c
   2. a
   3. d
   4. b

Chapter 11

EARLY ADULTHOOD: PHYSICAL, COGNITIVE, AND PERSONALITY DEVELOPMENT

CHAPTER OUTLINE

Influences on Adult Development
    Perceived Age
Youth: An Optional Period
Physical Development
Cognitive Development
    Beyond Formal Operations
        Problem Finding
        Dialectical Thought
        Contextual Model of Adult Cognition
        Characteristics of Mature Adult Thought
    Moral Development
        Criticisms of Kohlberg's Theory
Personality and Adjustment
    Developmental Tasks of Early Adulthood
    Life Events and Adjustments
        Timing and Sequencing of Life Events
Identity
    Identity Statuses in Early Adulthood
        Correlates of Identity Statuses
        Developmental Aspects of Adult Identity
Intimacy
    Intimacy and Attachment
    Sexual Intimacy
    Nonsexual Intimacy

SUMMARY OF KEY CONCEPTS

1.   Adult development is influenced by age-normative events, nonnormative events, and historical events. The impact of these influences varies across the lifespan.

2.   Early adulthood is a time of great diversity; young adults may be students or parents or jobholders or a combination of these. Young adults may stay in school or live at home until their late twenties.

3.   In early adulthood people are at their biological and physiological peak. The ability to perform cognitive tasks that require quick response time, short-term memory, and perception in complex relations is at its sharpest.

4.   Recent research suggests that the period of formal operations may not develop until late adolescence. Some investigators speculate that there is a cognitive

stage beyond formal operations, which is referred to as the *postformal stage*. In this stage thinking is relativistic; contradiction is seen as an inherent aspect of reality; and contradictory knowledge is integrated into higher-order systems of knowledge.

5. Adults consider the context and practical implications of an event. They may interpret situations differently on the basis of their experiences.

6. Moral development requires both cognitive development and personal experience. In youth and young adulthood, challenges to one's values and ideology are likely to influence moral reasoning and behavior.

7. Personality development in adulthood is affected by the accomplishment of specific developmental tasks. Several researchers have suggested patterns or stages in the accomplishment of these tasks.

8. Patterns of adjustment in young adulthood are influenced by the types of events people experience during this time. Life-event theory suggests that both positive and negative life events are potentially stressful and require adjustment by the individual.

9. A major question for young adults is how they are to relate to society. This question is closely tied to the stabilization of ego identity. According to Marcia, there are four *identity statuses* in youth and young adulthood: *identity achiever*, *identity foreclosure*, *moratorium*, and *identity diffusion*.

10. Once people have established their own identities, a new kind of *intimacy* becomes possible--an adult intimacy based on mutuality. The opposite of intimacy is *isolation* due either to emotional disturbance or a moratorium state. Intimacy in nonsexual as well as sexual relationships can be fully realized at this time of life.

KEY TERMS AND PHRASES

perceived age
youth
problem finding
dialectical process
life event
identity statuses
identity achiever
identity foreclosure
moratorium
identity diffusion
intimacy
isolation

REVIEW QUESTIONS

1. What are the three main types of influences on adult development?

2. What is meant by the terms *perceived age* and *youth*?

3. Briefly describe the physical and physiological development of young adults.

4. Briefly describe the cognitive development of young adults.

5. Some theorists suggest that there is a fifth stage of cognitive development. What competencies are present in this proposed stage?

6. In what respects has Kohlberg's theory of moral development, especially the adult stages, been challenged?

7. What are some of the developmental tasks of early adulthood?

8. What is a life event? How are life events related to adult adjustment?

9. Name the four identity statuses proposed by Marcia.

10. What kind of intimacy becomes possible in early adulthood?

EXERCISES

1. List Gould's stages of adult development.

AGE	DEVELOPMENTAL CHANGE
Before 18	
18-22	
22-28	

29-34

Mid-30s

40s-early 50s

53-60

---

2. Indicate with an X the category into which each identity status falls. (A status may fall into two categories.)

STATUS	CRISIS/NO CRISIS	COMMITMENT/NO COMMITMENT
Identity foreclosed		
Identity diffused		
Identity achieved		
Moratorium		

QUIZ

<u>True or False</u>

F 1. In our society, a person is defined as an adult when he or she reaches the age of 18.

T 2. The term *perceived age* refers to how old a person feels.

F 3. Before becoming an adult, the individual must pass through the stage known as youth.

T 4. The period of early adulthood is one of optimal biological functioning.

F 5. Young adults are more likely to die from diseases than from violent causes.

F 6. Biologically speaking, the best age for a woman to become pregnant for the first time is in her late teens.

T 7. Short-term memory is at its peak during the early adult years.

F 8. With few exceptions, people reach the stage of formal operations by age 15.

T 9. According to Arlin, there is a fifth stage of cognitive development called problem finding.

T 10. Dialectical thinking can occur in any stage of cognitive development.

F 11. Adult thinking is less relativistic than that of adolescents.

T 12. In young adulthood people acquire a strong sense of right and wrong based on their own experiences.

T 13. Most researchers accept the first two levels of Kohlberg's theory.

F 14. According to Gould, the first developmental task of early adulthood is to make commitments to career and family.

T 15. Levinson suggests that each individual creates a "life structure" of interrelated social and occupational roles.

T 16. A life event is any event that requires a significant change in the individual's life pattern.

F 17. Older adults generally experience more, and more positive, life events than younger ones.

F 18. White men are more likely than black men to marry before completing their education.

T 19. In early adulthood individuals begin to stabilize their identity.

F 20. People who are indecisive about life decisions and values are said to be characterized by identity foreclosure.

F 21. Once a person enters a state of moratorium, identity adjustment is no longer possible.

T 22. As people enter adulthood they show considerable variation in identity development.

T 23. The process of attachment influences the frequency and quality of interpersonal relationships throughout life.

__F__ 24. In a pseudointimate relationship the partner is treated more or less as a sexual object.

__F__ 25. Young adults tend to choose friends who remind them of themselves or what they want to be.

Sentence Completion

1. _AGE NORMATIVE_ influences on adult development include biological and maturational growth.

2. Young people who take a long time to "settle down" are said to have entered an optional period of development called _YOUTH_

3. According to Yankelovich, young people are more concerned with self-_fulfillment_ than with self-_SACRIFICE_

4. During early adulthood most people reach their full _HEIGHT_ but not their maximum _WEIGHT_.

5. Young adults are more likely to die from _ACCIDENTS_, _SUICIDE_, or _HOMICIDE_ than from diseases.

6. For women, _REPRODUCTIVE_ capacity is at its peak during young adulthood.

7. Tasks requiring quick _RESPONSE TIME_, _SHORT TERM_ memory, and the ability to perceive _COMPLEX_ relations are performed most efficiently during the late teens and early twenties.

8. In later writings Piaget suggested that the period of formal operations may not develop until _LATE_ _ADOLESCENE_ or _YOUNG ADULTHOOD_.

9. Some researchers argue that a person's _COGNITIVE STYLE_, or habitual pattern of approaching problem solving, affects performance on tasks measuring formal operations.

10. Arlin has identified a fifth stage of cognitive development termed _PROBLEM FINDING_.

11. According to Riegel, youths and young adults engage the world through a _DIALECTICAL_ process.

12. Some experts believe that thought that includes a consideration of the _CONTEXT_ and _IMPLICATIONS_ of an event is more sophisticated than formal-operational thought.

13. A feature of adult thought is the ability to integrate contradictory knowledge into more inclusive wholes or _METASYSTEMS_

14. Kohlberg has argued that one must reach the _FORMAL OPERATIONAL_ level of cognitive development before one can engage in postconventional moral reasoning.

15. According to Murphy and Gilligan, the _ABSOLUTIST_ of adolescent logic gives way to a more _RELATIVISTIC_ approach to moral dilemmas during young adulthood.

16. According to Gould, between the ages of 18 and 22 the main developmental task is to leave the _FAMILY_ and establish a _PEER GROUP_ orientation.

17. At the most general level, a _LIFE EVENT_ is any experience that is deemed noteworthy or significant by the individual.

18. According to Lowenthal and colleagues, the impact of an event on an individual depends on his or her _PERCEPTION_ of the event.

19. Over the past few decades the timing and order of life events have become _LESS_ clear-cut.

20. The four patterns of resolution of the identity crises are referred to as _IDENTITY STATUSES_.

21. _IDENTITY DIFFUSE_ individuals are uncommitted to specific lifestyles or values and show no evidence of personal crisis with respect to these issues.

22. According to Waterman, people begin the development of identity in a state of _DIFFUSENESS_ and _CONFUSION_.

23. According to some developmental psychologists, the foundation of adult intimacy is early _ATTACHMENT_ bonds.

24. In Erikson's model, the opposite of intimacy is _ISOLATION_

25. In early adulthood other adults are no longer perceived in terms of parental _STEREOTYPES_

Multiple Choice

_C_ 1. Which of the following is an example of a nonnormative influence on development?
   a.   growing up during the Vietnam War
   b.   reaching puberty
   c.   changing jobs
   d.   all of the above

_B_ 2. How old a person feels is referred to as his or her
   a.   chronological age.
   b.   perceived age.
   c.   psychological age.
   d.   maturational age.

A 3. The period between the time a person is legally an adult and the time he or she undertakes adult work and family roles is termed
    a. youth.
    b. postadolescence.
    c. the preadult period.
    d. the moratorium stage.

A 4. Which of the following reaches its maximum point in the early twenties?
    a. height
    b. weight
    c. physical strength
    d. all of the above

C 5. Which of the following statements is *not* true?
    a. Young adults are the healthiest individuals in our society.
    b. Some health problems of later life can be discerned in early adulthood.
    c. Young adults are less susceptible to stress-related disorders than older adults.
    d. Young adults are less likely to practice preventive health habits than older adults.

B 6. Biologically speaking, the best age for a woman to become pregnant is in her
    a. late teens.
    b. early twenties.
    c. late twenties.
    d. early thirties.

D 7. Which of the following tasks are performed most efficiently during the late teens and early twenties?
    a. those requiring quick response time
    b. those requiring short-term memory
    c. those requiring the ability to perceive complex relations
    d. all of the above

C 8. Which stage of cognitive development is characterized by hypothetical reasoning and abstract thought?
    a. the preoperational stage
    b. the concrete-operational stage
    c. the formal-operational stage
    d. the postformal stage

D 9. According to Arlin, there is a fifth stage of cognitive development characterized by
    a. ability to reason logically.
    b. recognition and acceptance of contradiction.
    c. consideration of the practical implications of an event.
    d. ability to generate new and relevant questions about the world.

_B_ 10. Acceptance of contradictions as a basic property of reality is referred to as
   a.   problem finding.
   b.   dialectical thought.
   c.   hypothetical reasoning.
   d.   contextual awareness.

_A_ 11. Which of the following statements is *not* true?
   a.   Developmental theorists have identified a fifth stage of cognitive development known as the postformal stage.
   b.   Unlike adolescent thought, adult thinking is relativistic.
   c.   Mature adults realize that contradiction is an inherent aspect of reality.
   d.   The mature adult thinker can integrate potentially incompatible systems of belief.

_C_ 12. Recent research has shown that the most critical determinant of postconventional moral reasoning is
   a.   biological maturation.
   b.   educational attainment.
   c.   adult life experiences.
   d.   gender.

_D_ 13. Which of the following statements is *not* true?
   a.   Most researchers accept the first two levels of Kohlberg's theory.
   b.   Many people regress to earlier stages of moral reasoning.
   c.   Some researchers believe postconventional morality is based on a postformal level of reasoning.
   d.   Because of their socialization, women are unable to achieve the highest levels of moral reasoning.

_B_ 14. According to Gould, what is the primary developmental task in the period from age 22 to age 28?
   a.   escaping from parental control
   b.   making commitments to career and family
   c.   realigning life goals
   d.   accepting one's life as it is

_A_ 15. Levinson suggests that each adult creates a combination of social and occupational roles known as a (an)
   a.   life structure.
   b.   social paradigm.
   c.   personal fable.
   d.   identity status.

_D_ 16. Which of the following statements is true?
   a.   All life events are potentially stressful.
   b.   Young adults experience more life events than older adults do.
   c.   The occurrence of an event is less critical than the individual's perception of that event.
   d.   All of the above.

_A_ 17. Which of the following statements is _not_ true?
   a. Each person experiences the major life events in approximately the same order.
   b. Not being "on time" in adopting an adult role is likely to be stressful to the individual.
   c. In recent decades the timing of life events has become less clear-cut.
   d. Women are most likely to deviate from the expected timetable of life events in the area of childbearing.

_B_ 18. A young man who enters his father's business because it is expected of him is an example of which of the following?
   a. identity achievement
   b. identity foreclosure
   c. identity diffusion
   d. moratorium

_D_ 19. Which of the following statements is _not_ true?
   a. People begin the development of identity in a state of diffuseness.
   b. An individual can move from a state of foreclosure to one of moratorium.
   c. A person who has reached the level of moratorium may either progress to identity achievement or regress to a state of diffuseness.
   d. Once an individual has reached the state of identity achievement, no further development of ego identity takes place.

_C_ 20. Which of the following has been found to contribute most to the development of ego identity?
   a. emphasis on propriety
   b. respect for scholarship
   c. focus on societal issues
   d. emphasis on practicality

_C_ 21. Which of the following statements is _not_ true?
   a. Intimacy is critical throughout development.
   b. Intimacy between two equal persons becomes possible in the early adult years.
   c. One must resolve the identity crisis before one can become intimate with another.
   d. Intimacy in females is closely tied to interpersonal relationships in general.

_A_ 22. According to some developmental psychologists, the foundation of adult intimacy is
   a. the attachment bonds of infants.
   b. the peer group relations of middle childhood.
   c. the sexual experimentation of adolescence.
   d. none of the above.

_B_ 23. A relationship that is based largely on convenience is referred to as
    a. intimate.
    ⓑ pseudointimate.
    c. stereotyped.
    d. devitalized.

_D_ 24. In Erikson's model, the opposite of intimacy is
    a. exploitation.
    b. diffuseness.
    c. mistrust.
    ⓓ isolation.

_C_ 25. In early adulthood nonsexual intimacy becomes possible as a result of
    a. the attainment of postconventional levels of morality.
    b. cognitive maturation.
    ⓒ the freeing of relationships from childhood expectations.
    d. the resolution of the identity crisis.

Matching

A. Influences on adult development:

_A_ 1. Age-normative influences   a. Biological and maturational growth
_C_ 2. History-normative influences   b. Important events that can occur at any time in life.
_B_ 3. Nonnormative influences   c. Major events like wars and epidemics.

B. Levinson's life structures:

_D_ 1. Novice phase   a. The time when people establish their initial way of living.
_E_ 2. Early adult transition   b. The time when people reappraise their earlier life.
_A_ 3. Entry life structure   c. The time when a person may search for a better life structure.
      for early adulthood
_B_ 4. Age 30 transition   d. The time when people begin to build a life structure.
_F_ 5. Culminating life structure   e. The bridge between preadulthood and adulthood.
      for early adulthood
_C_ 6. Midlife transition   f. The time when people seek to realize the goals set in their early 20s.

C. Identity statuses:

_D_ 1. Identity foreclosed   a. Struggling to achieve consistency about who one is and where one is going.

_C_ 2. Identity diffused   b. Has experienced crisis and reached a decision.

_B_ 3. Identity achieved   c. Not committed to a specific lifestyle or experiencing crisis.

_A_ 4. Moratorium   d. Has made lifestyle decisions without experiencing crisis.

ANSWERS

True or False

1. F
2. T
3. F
4. T
5. F
6. F
7. T
8. F
9. T
10. T
11. F
12. T
13. T
14. F
15. T
16. T
17. F
18. F
19. T
20. F
21. F
22. T
23. T
24. F
25. F

Sentence Completion

1. age-normative
2. youth
3. fulfillment, sacrifice
4. height, weight

5. accidents, suicide, homicide
6. reproductive
7. response time, short-term, complex
8. late adolescence, young adulthood
9. cognitive style
10. problem finding
11. dialectical
12. context, implications
13. metasystems
14. formal-operational
15. absolutist, relativistic
16. family, peer-group
17. life event
18. perception
19. less
20. identity statuses
21. identity-diffuse
22. diffuseness, confusion
23. attachment
24. isolation
25. stereotypes

Multiple Choice

1. c
2. b
3. a
4. a
5. c
6. b
7. d
8. c
9. d
10. b

11. a
12. c
13. d
14. b
15. a
16. d
17. a
18. b
19. d
20. c
21. c
22. a
23. b
24. d
25. c

Matching

A. 1. a
   2. c
   3. b

B. 1. d
   2. e
   3. a
   4. b
   5. f
   6. c

C. 1. d
   2. c
   3. b
   4. a

Chapter 12

EARLY ADULTHOOD:
FAMILY AND OCCUPATIONAL DEVELOPMENT

CHAPTER OUTLINE

Family Life
    Family Life Cycle
        Family Life-Cycle Models
        Limitations of Family Life-Cycle Models
        Nature and Function of the Family
    Marriage
        Mate Selection
        Courtship
    Marital Adjustment
        Sexual Adjustment
        Marital Roles and Work Roles
    Divorce
    Nonmarital Lifestyles
        Cohabitation
        Singlehood
        Homosexual Lifestyle
    Parenting
        Fertility Motivation
        Adjustment to Parenthood
Occupational Development
    Stage Theories
        Super's Theory of Occupational Development
        Levinson's Theory of Occupational Development
    Career Choice, Self-Concept, and Gender-Role Identity
    Two-Provider Families

SUMMARY OF KEY CONCEPTS

1.   The *family life cycle* begins at marriage and ends with the death of the remaining spouse. Family life cycle models are useful for describing changes in traditional families, but they do not explain changes in nontraditional families, nor do they acknowledge *intergenerational relations*.

2.   Social scientists define families structurally (in terms of who the family members are and how they are related to one another) and functionally (in terms of family activities and the role the family plays in the lives of its members).

3.   The age at which people marry and the way they marry are influenced by social norms. Some of the factors affecting the courtship process are physical attractiveness, propinquity, similarity in background and values, achievement of

rapport, mutual self-disclosure, role-taking ability, and the fitting together of roles and needs.

4. A newly married couple must learn to deal with conflict in a mature way and to make adjustments in the areas of money, sex, relatives, and the possibility of children. Most young people today prefer a marital relationship in which responsibilities are shared.

5. Most divorces occur within the first seven years of marriage. After a divorce, people seem to need to rework their lives and identities.

6. Although most Americans marry at least once, cohabitation is increasingly common. Some people remain single throughout much or all of their young adulthood. In addition, a growing number of men and women are living homosexual lifestyles.

7. In Erikson's model of development, parenthood emerges in response to the crisis of *generativity*. However, some people choose to resolve this crisis through their work.

8. The birth of a child restricts parental activities and privacy, imposes a financial burden on the family, and often disrupts the wife's career. Research indicates that marital satisfaction decreases with the advent of the first child, but that if children are wanted and planned for, they can strengthen a marriage.

9. People enter the work world during young adulthood and begin the process of moving up the occupational ladder. According to both Super and Levinson, occupational development can be conceptualized as a series of stages, each with its unique tasks or issues.

10. Initial job choice is influenced by many factors, including self-concept and gender-role identity. Entrance into many occupations is less gender determined than it once was.

11. Families with two providers are finding that there are many costs as well as benefits associated with this lifestyle. Personal motivation for working and job satisfaction are important factors in the adjustment of these families.

KEY TERMS AND PHRASES

family life cycle
intergenerational relations
stimulus-value-role theory
generativity
fertility motivation
role overload

REVIEW QUESTIONS

1. Briefly describe the family life cycle. How useful is this concept?

2. How do social scientists define the family?

3. What factors affect the selection of a mate?

4. In what respects must a newly married couple adjust to marriage?

5. What are the consequences of divorce for most people?

6. Briefly describe three frequently encountered nonmarital lifestyles.

7. What are some of the reasons that couples decide to have children?

8. What effects is the arrival of a child likely to have on a couple?

9. List the stages in Super's and Levinson's theories of occupational development.

10. What factors affect the choice of a first job?

11. What are the costs and benefits associated with two-provider families?

EXERCISES

1. List the stages in Hill's model of the family life cycle.

STAGE	DESCRIPTION
I	
II	

III _____

IV _____

V _____

VI _____

VII _____

VIII _____

IX _____

2. Briefly describe the stages in Super's and Levinson's models of occupational development.

STAGE	SUPER	LEVINSON
1		
2		
3		
4		
5		

QUIZ

<u>True or False</u>

_T_ 1. The family life cycle begins with marriage and ends when the surviving spouse dies.

_T_ 2. Duvall's model of the family life cycle ignores the impact of later-born children.

_F_ 3. Family life cycle models are useful in describing changes in nontraditional families.

_F_ 4. The average age at first marriage is lower today than it has ever been.

_T_ 5. Within the family, children are the primary targets of socialization.

_F_ 6. Today people no longer worry about getting married "on time."

_F_ 7. The best predictor of mutual liking between new acquaintances is propinquity.

_T_ 8. The term *homogamy* refers to the practice of choosing a mate who is similar to oneself.

_F_ 9. According to Murstein, the first stage of courtship is the value comparison stage.

_T_ 10. The majority of both men and women are not virgins when they marry.

_T_ 11. About half of all married men commit adultery.

_F_ 12. Husbands whose wives are employed spend about as much time on household tasks as their wives.

_T_ 13. One of the best predictors of divorce is age at first marriage.

_F_ 14. A person who has just experienced divorce tends to refrain from sexual intimacy for about a year.

_T_ 15. In contrast to the 1970s, cohabitation became less common in the 1980s.

_T_ 16. The average length of a cohabitation arrangement is eighteen months.

_F_ 17. Research findings confirm that most homosexuals are promiscuous and unable to form lasting intimate relationships.

_T_ 18. According to Erikson, after an individual has resolved the crisis of intimacy versus isolation he or she must resolve the crisis of generativity versus stagnation.

_F_ 19. The term *fertility motivation* refers to a couple's decisions about the wife's career.

_F_ 20. Marital satisfaction increases with the advent of the first child.

_T_ 21. According to Super, the first stage of occupational development is crystallization of one's ideas about work.

_F_ 22. According to Levinson, it is crucial to have created a life structure by the age of 25.

_T_ 23. A full-time job can be viewed as an implementation of the individual's self-concept.

_F_ 24. Today, couples with children are more likely to place career interests above family concerns.

_T_ 25. Women for whom work is a means of self-expression are more likely to succeed in integrating work and family roles than women who work primarily for financial reasons.

Sentence Completion

1. The most popular and enduring of all known social groupings is the _FAMILY_

2. Almost _HALF_ of the family life cycle occurs after the children are gone.

3. _STRUCTURAL_ definitions of the family focus on the pattern of organization that characterizes this societal unit.

4. Families are the context for _legitimate_ procreation.

5. Adults in families experience indirect _socialization_ as they interact with each other and with their offspring.

6. The age at which people marry for the first time has _risen_ since the last generation.

7. Three factors influence the mate selection process: _propinquity_, _homogamy_, and _physical attractiveness_.

8. Murstein's theory of marital choice is known as the _stimulus - value - role_ theory.

9. According to Murstein, the most important factor in a successful relationship is _equity_ in the rewarding power of the partners.

10. Sex, like other social behavior, is _learned_

11. Most couples find _extramarital_ sex unacceptable.

12. A crucial factor in the success of dual-earner families in sharing their work is the _gender role_ attitude of the spouses.

13. First marriages of women over ___30___ are the most stable.

14. A divorced person is likely to encounter an ___*identity crisis*___ in the course of building a new lifestyle.

15. An increasingly common lifestyle is ___*cohabitation*___, in which an unmarried couple live together and maintain a sexual relationship.

16. Most couples who live together believe that ___*parenthood*___ is reserved for marital relationships.

17. Single people tend to live in ___*urban centers*___.

18. Some homosexuals form ___*close couples*___ that resemble marriage.

19. The term ___*fertility motivation*___ refers to a couple's reasons for having or not having children.

20. The transition to parenthood has been described as a ___*crisis point*___ in the life of the couple.

21. According to Super, as people go through the stages of vocational development there is a continual ___*updating*___ and ___*implementing*___ of self-concept.

22. There has been no systematic long-term study of ___*women's*___ occupational development.

23. Young people today find that entrance into many occupations is determined less by ___*gender*___ than it used to be.

24. The most important reason for the rise of two-provider families is ___*finance*___.

25. For employed women who cannot afford child care and housekeeping support, the period of early adulthood is often marked by ___*task overload*___.

Multiple Choice

___B___ 1. The family life cycle begins with
   a. courtship.
   (b.) marriage.
   c. the birth of the first child.
   d. the establishment of a permanent residence.

___A___ 2. A definition of the family that specifies who family members are and how they are related to one another is a
   (a.) structural definition.
   b. psychological definition.
   c. functional definition.
   d. none of the above.

146

C 3. Which of the following is *not* a function of the family?
   a. caring for children
   b. providing companionship
   c. producing goods and services
   d. socializing children and adults

D 4. The best predictor of mutual liking between new acquaintances is
   a. propinquity.
   b. similarity in education.
   c. shared values.
   d. physical attractiveness.

C 5. According to Murstein, the first stage of courtship is the
   a. role stage.
   b. value comparison stage.
   c. stimulus stage.
   d. equity stage.

B 6. In the past few decades there has been a dramatic increase in premarital sexual behavior among
   a. men.
   b. women.
   c. homosexuals.
   d. all of the above.

A 7. Sexual activity is most frequent among
   a. newly married couples.
   b. couples married more than 15 years.
   c. recently engaged couples.
   d. couples who have decided to have a child.

C 8. Which of the following statements is *not* true?
   a. Married women who are not employed tend to be more passive than employed wives.
   b. Employed wives experience more marital satisfaction than wives who do not work outside the home.
   c. Husbands of employed women tend to be more dominant than husbands of homemakers.
   d. Stress is most likely to appear during transition periods, such as when a wife enters the labor force.

B 9. What proportion of couples who marry today can be expected to divorce?
   a. about one-quarter
   b. more than one out of three
   c. almost half
   d. more than half

_D_ 10. Which of the following is a typical reaction to divorce?
   a. depression
   b. problems of identity
   c. sexual experimentation
   (d.) all of the above

_D_ 11. Nonlegal marital cohabitation is cohabitation in which the partners
   a. cannot legally marry because they are of the same sex or are married to others.
   b. are living together as part of the courtship process.
   c. share living quarters for financial or other reasons.
   (d.) are committed to each other and intend to have children.

_A_ 12. What proportion of men are single at the age of 25?
   (a.) about 33 percent
   b. over 25 percent
   c. 22 percent
   d. about 15 percent

_C_ 13. The term *dysfunctionals* is applied to homosexuals who
   a. live a "single" life arranged around homosexual activities.
   b. are older and have difficulty forming intimate relationships.
   (c.) live alone and are troubled by their homosexuality.
   d. live with other homosexuals and are committed to the relationship.

_B_ 14. In Erikson's model, parenthood emerges in response to the crisis of generativity versus
   a. isolation.
   (b.) stagnation.
   c. intimacy.
   d. role confusion.

_D_ 15. The most frequently cited reason for having children is
   a. "for the fun and stimulation children bring."
   b. "to be able to influence or control someone."
   c. "because it is the morally correct thing to do."
   (d.) "to expand myself, have someone to follow me."

_A_ 16. Which of the following statements is _not_ true?
   (a.) For most couples the birth of the first child is not a stressful event.
   b. The arrival of an infant restricts the parents' activities outside the home.
   c. Marital satisfaction decreases with the advent of the first child.
   d. The status of parenthood leads to new relationships between the couple and society.

_C_ 17. For most men and women, identity is closely tied to
   a. education.
   b. parenthood.
   (c.) occupation.
   d. religion.

_D_ 18. In Super's model of occupational development, the period from age 24 to age 35 is characterized by
   a.   specification of an occupational preference.
   b.   consolidation and advancement within a field.
   c.   implementation of one's training.
   (d.) stabilization and development of a job reputation.

_B_ 19. According to Levinson, between the ages of 28 and 32 many men experience a
   a.   midlife crisis.
   (b.) transitional period.
   c.   crystallization of their ideas about work.
   d.   sense of failure and futility.

_A_ 20. For women, the most important factor in long-term career success is
   (a.) working continuously.
   b.   obtaining an advanced degree.
   c.   having only one child.
   d.   avoiding male bias.

_C_ 21. Which of the following statements is _not_ true?
   a.   There is a high correlation between people's self-concept and their images of the occupations to which they aspire.
   b.   Reevaluation of the match between one's career and self-concept can take place at any point in the life cycle.
   (c.) Entrance into many occupations continues to be based almost entirely on gender.
   d.   Women who do not conform to gender-role stereotypes tend to experience some social and interpersonal stresses.

_A_ 22. What proportion of married women with children under 18 are employed?
   (a.) 52 percent
   b.   43 percent
   c.   38 percent
   d.   33 percent

_B_ 23. Women who work outside the home yet still do most of the housework may suffer from
   a.   gender confusion.
   (b.) role overload.
   c.   marital stagnation.
   d.   midlife crisis.

_D_ 24. Women who return to work after having children are more likely to be successful if they
   a.   can trust others to care for their children.
   b.   view work as an avenue of self-expression.
   c.   are not experiencing financial strain.
   (d.) all of the above.

C 25. Which of the following statements is *not* true?
- a. Families in which both spouses work have additional financial security.
- b. Working tends to broaden a person's social network.
- c. Employment does not affect a woman's self-esteem.
- d. Employed women report greater life satisfaction than unemployed women.

Matching

A. Murstein's stages of marital choice:

C 1. Stimulus stage   a. Planning for marriage.
B 2. Value comparison stage   b. Gathering information.
A 3. Role stage   c. Forming initial impressions.

B. Homosexual life patterns:

D 1. Close couples
E 2. Open couples
B 3. Functionals
A 4. Dysfunctionals
C 5. Asexuals

- a. Live alone and are troubled by their homosexuality.
- b. Live a "single" life arranged around homosexual activities.
- c. Are sexually inactive and have difficulty forming intimate relationships.
- d. Have intimate relationships that resemble marriage.
- e. Live with other homosexuals but are not committed to the relationship.

C. Super's theory of occupational development:

A 1. Crystallization
C 2. Specification
E 3. Implementation
D 4. Stabilization
B 5. Consolidation

- a. Comparison of possible career paths.
- b. Peak earning power.
- c. Determining an occupational preference.
- d. Developing a job reputation.
- e. Adoption of the worker role.

ANSWERS

True or False

1. T
2. T
3. F
4. F
5. T
6. F

150

7. F
8. T
9. F
10. T
11. T
12. F
13. T
14. F
15. F
16. T
17. F
18. T
19. F
20. F
21. T
22. F
23. T
24. F
25. T

Sentence Completion

1. family
2. half
3. structural
4. legitimate
5. socialization
6. risen
7. physical attractiveness, propinquity, homogamy
8. stimulus-value-role theory
9. equity
10. learned
11. extramarital
12. gender role
13. 30
14. identity crisis
15. cohabitation
16. parenthood
17. urban centers
18. close couples
19. fertility motivation
20. crisis point
21. updating, implementing
22. women's
23. gender
24. financial need
25. task overload

Multiple Choice

1. b
2. a
3. c
4. d
5. c
6. b
7. a
8. c
9. b
10. d
11. d
12. a
13. c
14. b
15. d
16. a
17. c
18. d
19. b
20. a
21. c
22. a
23. b
24. d
25. c

Matching

A. 1. c
   2. b
   3. a

B. 1. d
   2. e
   3. b
   4. a
   5. c

C. 1. a
   2. c
   3. e
   4. d
   5. b

Chapter 13

MIDDLE ADULTHOOD: PHYSICAL, COGNITIVE, AND PERSONALITY DEVELOPMENT

CHAPTER OUTLINE

SUMMARY OF KEY CONCEPTS

1. Middle age is characterized by a gradual physical decline. Physical strength is replaced by judgment, experience, and management ability.

2. In middle age concerns about physical health become more common. Cardio-vascular diseases and cancer are the two leading causes of death during this time. Stressful life events can contribute to health problems. Emotional and personality factors--particularly *Type A behavior*--are major contributors to the health problems of middle-aged adults.

3. One effect of aging is the *climacteric*, the changes in the reproductive and sexual organs that result from a decrease in the production of gonadal hormones. For women, this biological change is evident in *menopause*, in which menstruation gradually ceases over a period of a year or two. For men, the results of reduced hormone production are less clear-cut.

4. Cognitive development continues in middle age in abilities that are influenced by experience, such as verbal ability, social knowledge, and moral judgment. Longitudinal research does not show a decline in intelligence in middle age.

5. Some theorists propose that intelligence has two components: *fluid* abilities, which peak in early adulthood and are related to neurophysiological intactness, and *crystallized* abilities, which are a result of acculturation and remain unchanged or even increase during middle age.

6. Creativity, as measured by products, declines with age. Divergent thinking and preference for complexity also decline with age and may contribute to the decline in creativity. Different kinds of creativity may emerge at different ages.

7. It is difficult to determine whether adult personality is basically stable or whether people undergo major personality changes across the lifespan. Some theorists have suggested that the individual's basic personality structure remains essentially the same but that the behaviors representing that structure may change.

8. Most theorists believe that middle age is a time of challenge for the individual. It may require considerable adjustment in such areas as the self, family relations, social interactions, career development, and leisure activity.

9. Erikson sees the midlife crisis as one of *generativity* (concern for the next generation) versus *stagnation* (a sense of boredom and preoccupation with the self). Other views of development in middle adulthood have been proposed by Peck, Havighurst, and Levinson.

KEY TERMS AND PHRASES

presbycusis
Type-A behavior
climacteric
menopause
osteoporosis
crystallized intelligence
fluid intelligence
genotypic continuity
phenotypic continuity
generativity
stagnation

REVIEW QUESTIONS

1. Briefly describe the physical changes that occur in middle adulthood.

2. How does stress affect health during middle adulthood?

3. What is Type-A behavior?

4. What is meant by the climacteric? How does it differ in men and women?

5. How does sexuality in middle adulthood differ from the sexuality of youth?

6. What changes in intellectual functioning occur during middle adulthood?

7. What is meant by fluid and crystallized abilities?

8. What factors contribute to an apparent decline in creativity with age?

9. What effects, if any, does aging have on the personality?

10. What are the developmental tasks of middle adulthood?

EXERCISES

1. List the seven personal habits that are related to the health status and longevity of older adults.

2. Briefly summarize the four main theories about the developmental tasks of middle adulthood.

Erikson

_____

Peck

_____

Havighurst

_____

Levinson

_____

QUIZ

<u>True or False</u>

_F_ 1. The transition from young adulthood to middle adulthood is generally agreed to occur at age 30.

_T_ 2. The percentage of body weight that is fat increases in middle adulthood.

_F_ 3. At about age 35 the human organism experiences a reversal from growth to deterioration.

_F_ 4. Aging is a strictly biological process.

_T_ 5. Moderate alcohol consumption is positively associated with good health.

_T_ 6. Marriage and the birth of a child are among the most stressful life events.

_F_ 7. Certain life events, such as divorce, are inherently stressful.

_T_ 8. Impatience with delay and excessive competitiveness are characteristic of Type-A behavior.

_F_ 9. People who exhibit Type-B behaviors are at greater risk of suffering a heart attack than Type-A individuals.

_T_ 10. The average age at menopause is 50.

_T_ 11. Osteoporosis is a condition in which bones become thinner and more breakable.

_F_ 12. Unlike women, men do not experience a climacteric.

_F_ 13. Sexual satisfaction declines dramatically during middle adulthood.

_T_ 14. Cognitive development continues during middle adulthood.

_F_ 15. Intelligence test scores are at their highest between the ages of 35 and 45.

_F_ 16. Crystallized intelligence relates to abilities such as drawing inferences about relationships and comprehending their implications.

_T_ 17. Fluid intelligence peaks between the ages of 20 and 30 and thereafter declines.

_T_ 18. Artists reach their peak creativity earlier than scientists and scholars.

_F_ 19. Recent research has found that the capacity for divergent thinking declines steadily from young adulthood on.

_T_ 20. Genotypic continuity refers to the stability of an underlying personality structure.

_F_ 21. Relative stability refers to whether people maintain the same score, or level of functioning, from one evaluation to another.

_T_ 22. Much research evidence supports the assumption of personality stability in adulthood.

_T_ 23. Of the personality dimensions studied by Haan, those most directly concerned with the self tended to be the most stable.

_F_ 24. According to Erikson, during middle adulthood people must resolve the crisis of intimacy versus isolation.

_F_ 25. Theories of adult development tend to view middle-aged adults as a fairly homogeneous group.

Sentence Completion

1. Muscular strength declines _slowly_ and _steadily_ from young adulthood onward.

2. During middle age there appears to be a slowing of _conductivity_ in the peripheral nerves and across synapses.

3. _Atherosclerosis_ is a degenerative condition involving thickening and hardening of the artery walls.

4. The most common auditory problem associated with increasing age is _presbycusis_.

5. It has long been recognized that an individual's rate of physical decline is partly determined by _heredity_

6. For middle-aged and older adults, the most important health habit may be _a proper diet_.

7. Researchers have found a positive relationship between the incidence of heart attacks and the number and type of _stressful life events_.

8. For employed parents or dual-earner families, a common source of stress during middle adulthood is _role_ _conflicts_

9. The _Type A_ behavior pattern includes accelerated speech, impatience with delay, excessive competitiveness, restlessness, and undue irritability.

10. During middle adulthood people undergo a set of changes in their reproductive organs known as the _climacteric_ .

11. In women, the decrease in estrogen levels eventually leads to _menopause_, or cessation of menses.

12. A long-term effect of a decreased level of estrogen is _osteoporosis_, a condition in which bones become thinner and more fragile.

13. At about age 50 men experience a decline in _testosterone_ levels.

14. To some extent, sexual expression in midlife is influenced by _cultural expectations_

15. Recent research has suggested that intellectual development _continues_ in middle adulthood.

16. A problem with _cross sectional_ research is that we cannot assume that the differences between age groups are solely a result of aging.

17. _Crystallized_ intelligence is a result of accumulated knowledge and problem-solving techniques.

18. _Fluid_ intelligence peaks between the ages of 20 and 30 and thereafter declines.

19. Studies of creativity have found that _artists_ reach their peak productivity earlier than _scientists_ and _scholars_

20. It appears that a positive view of _the self_ is a motivating factor underlying a person's desire to seek creative solutions to problems.

21. Some writers use the term _middlescence_ to account for a troubled midlife passage.

22. Much of the research evidence supports the assumption of personality _stability_ in adulthood.

23. According to Haan, personality development is characterized by a moderate degree of *relative stability*

24. According to Erikson, the central crisis for middle-aged adults is one of *generativity* versus *stagnation*.

25. Each theory of adult development sees middle age as a time of continued *challenge* for the individual.

Multiple Choice

D 1. The transition from young adulthood to middle adulthood occurs at
  a.   age 30.
  b.   age 40.
  c.   age 50.
  d.   any age; it depends on the individual.

C 2. The most obvious signs of physical aging are manifested in
  a.   hearing.
  b.   the bones.
  c.   the skin and hair.
  d.   breathing efficiency.

A 3. Which of the following statements is *not* true?
  a.   At about age 30 the human organism shifts from growth to deterioration.
  b.   Nerve cells do not multiply after the first year of life.
  c.   The heart diseases of middle age are a result of cumulative conditions.
  d.   The shift from growth to decline is inevitable.

D 4. Which of the following is a significant influence on an individual's rate of physical decline?
  a.   heredity
  b.   environmental factors
  c.   marital status
  d.   all of the above

B 5. Which of the following personal habits is *not* related to longevity?
  a.   regular exercise
  b.   avoiding alcoholic beverages
  c.   eating at mealtimes
  d.   sleeping 7 to 9 hours a night

B 6. On Holmes and Rahe's Social Readjustment Scale, a significant decline in health is likely to occur if the person scores over
  a.   500.
  b.   300.
  c.   100.
  d.   10.

C 7. Which of the following statements is *not* true?
   a. Ordinary everyday hassles can contribute to the level of stress experienced by an individual.
   b. Role conflicts are a common source of stress for employed parents.
   c. Certain life events are stressful for everyone.
   d. A person's stress level is influenced by his or her coping methods.

A 8. Which of the following is *not* a characteristic of Type-A behavior?
   a. low-to-moderate achievement striving
   b. accelerated speech
   c. impatience with delay
   d. restlessness

C 9. After menopause sexual activity often becomes
   a. impossible.
   b. painful.
   c. more satisfying.
   d. none of the above.

B 10. A condition in which bones become thinner and more fragile is known as
   a. presbycusis.
   b. osteoporosis.
   c. atheroslerosis.
   d. cystic fibrosis.

C 11. The male climacteric is marked by a decrease in the production of
   a. estrogen.
   b. progesterone.
   c. testosterone.
   d. all of the above.

D 12. Which of the following statements is true?
   a. Sexual desire decreases markedly in middle adulthood. F
   b. The reported frequency of marital intercourse among people over 35 has decreased since the 1950s. F
   c. People over 50 cannot safely ignore birth control. F
   d. None of the above.

A 13. At what age do intelligence test scores seem to peak?
   a. 25-35
   b. 35-45
   c. 45-55
   d. none of the above

D 14. Members of different generations have different experiences that may affect their intelligence. The effect of such differences can be minimized by
   a. cohort studies.
   b. cross-sectional research.
   c. standardized testing.
   d. longitudinal studies.

159

B 15. Which of the following is an example of fluid intelligence?
- a. ability to speak a language
- b. ability to put a puzzle together
- c. ability to solve problems
- d. none of the above

A 16. Which of the following increases with age?
- a. crystallized intelligence
- b. native intelligence
- c. fluid intelligence
- d. creative intelligence

C 17. Which of the following statements is *not* true?
- a. Musicians appear to reach their peak productivity earlier than scientists.
- b. Creativity has been found to be related to a preference for complexity.
- c. Middle-aged adults perform less well than younger and older adults on divergent-thinking tasks.
- d. It appears that a positive view of the self underlies a person's willingness to seek creative solutions to problems.

D 18. The term *middlescence* refers to
- a. the climacteric.
- b. the tendency to stagnate in middle age.
- c. the decline of creativity in middle age.
- d. none of the above.

B 19. Which of the following terms refers to the degree of similarity in overt behavior at two different times?
- a. genotypic continuity
- b. phenotypic continuity
- c. relative stability
- d. absolute stability

A 20. Research on personality stability has found that adult personality
- a. remains stable over time.
- b. is highly changeable.
- c. changes gradually between the ages of 20 and 90.
- d. cannot be measured.

D 21. According to Haan, which of the following dimensions of personality tends to be less stable than the others?
- a. cognitive investment
- b. open versus closed self
- c. self confidence
- d. under- versus overcontrolled heterosexuality

B 22. According to Haan, personality development is characterized by
    a.   a high degree of absolute stability.
    (b.)   a moderate degree of relative stability.
    c.   low absolute stability and high relative stability.
    d.   none of the above.

B 23. In Erikson's theory, *generativity* refers to
    a.   having children.
    (b.)   guiding the next generation.
    c.   productivity in one's job.
    d.   all of the above.

C 24. Which of the following is *not* a developmental task identified by Robert Peck?
    a.   learning to value wisdom over strength
    b.   redefining relationships with others
    (c.)   maintaining satisfactory occupational performance
    d.   remaining mentally flexible

A 25. Levinson's theory of adult development emphasizes
    (a.)   the major transitions from one era to the next.
    b.   societal pressures on the individual.
    c.   the need to cope with changes both within and outside the person.
    d.   all of the above.

Matching

A. Physical conditions of middle adulthood:

D 1. atherosclerosis
C 2. presbycusis
A 3. cardiovascular disease
F 4. climacteric

B 5. menopause
E 6. osteoporosis

a. Heart disease.
b. Cessation of menses.
c. Progressive loss of hearing.
d. Thickening and hardening of the artery walls.
e. Thinning of the bones.
f. Changes in the reproductive organs.

B. Cognitive capacities of middle adulthood:

B 1. crystallized intelligence
D 2. fluid intelligence
A 3. divergent thinking
C 4. preference for complexity

a. Ability to think of many different ideas appropriate to a situation.
b. Accumulated knowledge and problem-solving techniques.
c. Ability to appreciate complex concepts.
d. Ability to see relationships, draw inferences, and comprehend implications.

C. Aspects of personality stability:

D 1. genotypic continuity   a. The degree of similarity in overt behavior at two different times.

A 2. phenotypic continuity   b. Whether a person maintains the same score from one evaluation to another.

C 3. relative stability   c. The ordered distribution of scores of subjects across a period of time.

B 4. absolute stability   d. The stability of an underlying personality structure or pattern of traits.

ANSWERS

True or False

1. F
2. T
3. F
4. F
5. T
6. T
7. F
8. T
9. F
10. T
11. T
12. F
13. F
14. T
15. F
16. F
17. T
18. T
19. F
20. T
21. F
22. T
23. T
24. F
25. F

4. presbycusis
5. heredity
6. a proper diet
7. stressful life events
8. role conflicts
9. Type-A
10. climacteric
11. menopause
12. osteoporosis
13. testosterone
14. cultural expectations
15. continues
16. cross sectional
17. crystallized
18. fluid
19. artists, scientists, scholars
20. the self
21. middlescence
22. stability
23. relative stability
24. generativity, stagnation
25. challenge

Sentence Completion

1. slowly, steadily
2. conductivity
3. atherosclerosis

Multiple Choice

1. d
2. c
3. a
4. d
5. b
6. b
7. c
8. a

9. c
10. b
11. c
12. d
13. a
14. d
15. b
16. a
17. c
18. d
19. b
20. a
21. d
22. b
23. d
24. c
25. a

Matching

A.
1. d
2. c
3. a
4. f
5. b
6. e

B.
1. b
2. d
3. a
4. c

C.
1. d
2. a
3. c
4. b

Chapter 14

MIDDLE ADULTHOOD:
FAMILY AND OCCUPATIONAL DEVELOPMENT

CHAPTER OUTLINE

Family Life
> Intergenerational Relations
>> Families with Adolescents
>> Families with Adult Children
>> Relationships with Aged Parents
>> Grandparenthood
> Marriage
>> Midlife Marital Adjustment
>> Marital Styles
>> Types of Marriages
>> Companionship and Marriage
>> Family Violence
>> Midlife Divorce
>> Widowhood
>> Singlehood

Occupational Development
> Occupational Advancement
>> Personality and Occupational Advancement
> Job Satisfaction
> Retraining and Second Careers
> Integrating Work and Leisure

SUMMARY OF KEY CONCEPTS

1. Intergenerational relations become increasingly significant during middle adulthood. The middle-aged adult is between two generations and therefore is influenced by both "top-down" and "bottom-up" family processes.

2. Before their children leave home, parents must deal with the conflicts encountered in raising adolescents. They must support adolescents in their search for identity, help them explore career options, and prepare them to take their places in the adult world.

3. For most parents, the "empty-nest" phase of the family life cycle represents freedom and is experienced as a relief. For some, however, the absence of their children is difficult to bear.

4. Relations between middle-aged parents and their adult children are closer than is generally assumed. Each relies on the other for support and psychological well-being.

5. A reversal of parent and child roles sometimes occurs in middle age, with the middle-aged child caring for and supporting aging, dependent parents. Most older people neither want nor need to be dependent on their children.

6. A person is likely to become a grandparent for the first time during middle age. Grandparents play an important role in the family system, offering emotional support, child care, and advice on basic values, lifestyle, occupation, and parenting, especially to single-parent families. Just as there are styles of parenting, so too are there styles of grandparenting.

7. Most research suggests that marital adjustment is high during middle adulthood, particularly in the postchild phase of the family life cycle. When problems do arise, they are often related to differential growth of the partners, finances, sexual boredom, and work pressures.

8. Some investigators suggest that the longer a couple remain together, the more likely it is that their relationship will be characterized by complementarity of roles. However, most research indicates that marital adjustment is linked to similarity in the partners' interests, attitudes, and personality. An especially important factor is the development of a companion relationship with one's spouse.

9. Millions of women are physically bettered by their husbands. Socialization practices that foster a dominant, assertive role in men and a submissive, passive role in women contribute to this situation.

10. Divorce in midlife is becoming increasingly common. As at other ages, midlife divorce is painful and is usually followed by loneliness, self-doubt, mood swings, and many readjustments.

11. Many women lose their husbands before the age of 60. Middle-aged widows must deal with such problems as meeting new male companions, starting new sexual relationships, maintaining old friendships, and adjusting to reduced finances.

12. For many adults, generativity is achieved on the job through the development of ideas, products, and plans, and by guiding others in their job development. In middle age most people are concerned with consolidating their work position and advancing. The traits that are most frequently associated with career success are intellectual competence, high achievement orientation, forcefulness, dominance, commitment, ambition, dependability, low hostility and self-defeating attitudes, and objectivity.

13. Technological advances have radically changed the work world and have resulted in the need for retraining for many middle-aged adults. Middle-aged workers who lost their jobs often face serious problems in finding new jobs.

14. In midlife, leisure activities are often pursued alone. Such activities often help people adapt to role changes and find satisfaction that may be absent in other areas of their lives.

KEY TERMS AND PHRASES

mentor relationships
generational stations
empty-nest syndrome
marital companionship

REVIEW QUESTIONS

1. In what ways does the nature of family life change during middle age?

2. What special tasks are faced by the parents of adolescents?

3. What changes in intergenerational relationships occur during middle adulthood?

4. Briefly describe the role of grandparents in family systems.

5. Why does marital satisfaction tend to increase during middle adulthood?

6. List the five types of marriage identified by Cuber and Harroff.

7. What special circumstances are associated with divorce in midlife?

8. What are some of the characteristics of occupational development in middle adulthood?

9. What factors are leading to an increase in the frequency of second careers?

10. How does the nature of leisure activity change in midlife?

EXERCISES

1. Describe the five styles of grandparenting identified by Neugarten and Weinstein.

STYLE	DESCRIPTION
Formal	
Fun-seeker	
Surrogate-parent	
Reservoir of family wisdom	
Distant figure	

2. Briefly describe the five basic types of marriage identified by Cuber and Harroff.

TYPE	DESCRIPTION
Conflict-habituated	
Devitalized	
Passive-congenial	
Vital	
Total	

QUIZ

<u>True or False</u>

F 1. The issue of generativity involves establishing a reputation and advancing in one's occupation.

F 2. For most couples, the majority of the family life cycle is occupied with raising children.

F 3. Once they move away from home, adult children rarely return.

T 4. Until recently social scientists showed little interest in intergenerational relations.

T 5. General political orientation tends to show cross-generational continuity.

T 6. Parents often assist their adolescent children in making career choices.

F 7. The relationship between parents and their adult children is similar to that between parents and their adolescent children.

F 8. Parent-child relationships become less voluntary in middle adulthood.

T 9. The empty-nest syndrome has become less common since the 1970s.

T 10. On the average, elderly people are better off financially than they were in the past.

F 11. Women typically become grandmothers around the age of 60.

T 12. The "formal" grandparenting style includes providing special gifts or services.

F 13. Most couples become progressively closer over the course of a marriage.

F 14. For a marriage to be successful, the partners must have the same interests and needs.

T 15. Marital satisfaction is highest in egalitarian couples.

F 16. The most important factor in marital satisfaction is sexual compatibility.

T 17. Over 25 million women are victims of wife beating.

T 18. About 15 percent of divorces occur after fifteen years of marriage.

F 19. People who divorce in midlife have great difficulty finding new partners.

T 20. Because women tend to outlive men, widowhood is becoming an almost universal phase of life.

_T_ 21. In midlife people are concerned with maintaining a satisfactory level in their career.

_F_ 22. Recent research has shown that college graduates do not advance significantly further than high school graduates.

_T_ 23. Working women score significantly higher on most measures of psychological well-being.

_F_ 24. Unemployment is relatively rare among middle-aged workers.

_F_ 25. Napping and taking a sauna are examples of developmental pleasures.

Sentence Completion

1. Relationships in which one trains and guides a younger employee are known as _MENTOR RELATIONSHIPS_

2. Most couples will spend _HALF_ of the family life cycle living together alone after the children have grown.

3. Research has shown that intergenerational relationships tend to be _BIDIRECTIONAL_

4. Research on religious values has found _HIGH_ similarity between parents and their adult children.

5. Middle-aged adults are the _LINK_ between the younger and older generations.

6. In addition to resolving conflicts between them and their growing children, middle-aged adults must come to terms with their own _INNER CONFLICTS_

7. Parents and their grown children are social _EQUALS_

8. Increasingly, parent-child interaction is part of _____ rather than part of _____.

9. The empty-nest syndrome is _LESS_ common today than it was in the early 1970s.

10. During middle adulthood there is sometimes a _REVERSAL_ of parent-child roles.

11. Grandparents provide younger generations with _EMOTIONAL SUPPORT_ and ~~CARE~~ _ADVICE_.

12. In the _SURROGATE PARENT_ style of grandparenting, a grandparent assumes child care responsibilities while the parents are working.

13. Recent studies show an _UPTURN_ in marital satisfaction in the later stages of married life.

14. Some researchers believe that marital adjustment depends on _SIMILARITY_ between the partners, while others believe that it depends on _COMPLIMENTARITY_

15. According to Cuber and Harroff, a _CONFLICT-HABITUATED_ marriage is characterized by considerable conflict and tension.

16. In a _PASSIVE-CONGENIAL_ marriage the couple are content and comfortable with what they have.

17. Wives who are beaten are likely to be _SOCIALLY CONDITIONED_ into the victim role.

18. Many midlife divorces are caused by differential _GROWTH_ of the marital partners.

19. Midlife divorce is usually followed by _MARRIAGE._

20. In the United States there are over _90,000_ under 60 years of age who are widowed.

21. Whereas achievement-oriented women are _MORE_ likely to remain single, achievement-oriented men are _LESS_ likely to do so.

22. Between the ages of 35 and 65, men's average yearly earnings are _NEARLY DOUBLE_ those of women.

23. In middle age most people are seeking some assurance of job _STABILITY._

24. Among the serious problems encountered by middle-aged workers are _JOB OBSOLESCENCE_, _UNEMPLOYMENT_, and _AGE . DISCRIMINATION_

25. _RELAXATION_ is the least intense form of leisure.

Multiple Choice

B 1. Situations in which an older worker trains and guides one or several younger employees are known as
    a. management seminars.
    (b) mentor relationships.
    c. retraining workshops.
    d. office cliques.

B 2. Most middle-aged couples are in which stage of the family life cycle?
    a. child rearing
    (b) launching
    c. empty nest
    d. none of the above

_C_ 3. Research on intergenerational relations has shown that intergenerational influences tend to be
   a. nonexistent.
   b. unidirectional.
   (c.) reciprocal.
   d. too complex for study.

_C_ 4. In which of the following areas is the youngest generation most likely to influence middle-aged parents?
   a. household management
   b. money matters
   (c) social attitudes
   d. religious values

_D_ 5. Which of the following statements is *not* true?
   a. Middle-aged parents must come to terms with their own inner conflicts.
   b. The independence and autonomy of adolescents is a sign of successful parenting.
   c. Parental assistance can be critical in an adolescent's choice of a career.
   (d.) It is usually a bad idea for grandparents to attempt to teach their adult children about infant development.

_D_ 6. Relationships between middle-aged parents and their adult children differ from earlier parent-child relationships in that
   a. parents and adult children are social equals.
   b. the emotional attachments of both parents and adult children are redirected.
   c. parent-child relationships become more voluntary.
   (d) all of the above.

_C_ 7. Which of the following statements is *not* true?
   a. Parent-child relationships remain important during middle adulthood.
   b. Adult children often rely on their parents for financial and emotional support.
   (c.) Middle-aged parents tend to feel threatened by the achievements of their children.
   d. Parents may experience considerable stress when their children grow up and leave home.

_A_ 8. The empty-nest syndrome is least likely to occur among
   (a.) employed women.
   b. older fathers.
   c. full-time homemakers.
   d. single parents.

B 9. Today middle-aged adults are most likely to provide which of the following to their aging parents?
    a. income maintenance
    b. emotional support
    c. health care
    d. housing

C 10. In our culture a person typically becomes a grandparent around the age of
    a. 30.
    b. 40.
    c. 50.
    d. 60.

A 11. In which of the following grandparenting styles does the grandparent expect mutually gratifying experiences with the grandchild?
    a. fun-seeker
    b. surrogate-parent
    c. reservoir of family wisdom
    d. distant figure

D 12. In the later stages of married life marital satisfaction tends to
    a. decline rapidly.
    b. decrease gradually.
    c. remain unchanged.
    d. improve.

A 13. In which of the following is marital satisfaction likely to be highest?
    a. egalitarian couples
    b. husband-dominant couples
    c. wife-dominant couples
    d. either b or c

B 14. In which of the following types of marriage do the partners believe they love each other even though their marriage has little passion or intimacy?
    a. conflict-habituated
    b. devitalized
    c. passive-congenial
    d. vital

B 15. The primary factor in marital satisfaction is
    a. sex.
    b. companionship.
    c. financial stability.
    d. good health.

16. Which of the following statements is *not* true?
    a. Up to 60 percent of all married women are subjected to physical violence by their husbands at some time.
    b. Women are likely to be socially conditioned into the victim role.
    c. Battered wives often stay with their husbands.
    d. Research has shown that women who are beaten provoke their husbands to behave violently.

17. Marital discord is likely to occur when
    a. the personality of one spouse changes while that of the other spouse does not.
    b. the personalities of the spouses change in opposite directions.
    c. the personalities of both spouses change in the same direction but at different rates.
    d. all of the above.

18. People who divorce in midlife
    a. are unlikely to remarry.
    b. sometimes remarry after several years.
    c. are likely to remarry within three years.
    d. may remarry, provided that the new spouse has been married before.

19. In contemporary society widowhood is increasingly associated with
    a. old age.
    b. middle age.
    c. young adulthood.
    d. none of the above--it is becoming less frequent.

20. which of the following statements is true?
    a. Never-married women are more achievement-oriented than single men.
    b. Older single women usually have never received a proposal of marriage.
    c. Successful men tend to remain single.
    d. None of the above.

21. During midlife people are concerned with
    a. reaching a satisfactory level in their career.
    b. reevaluating their career goals.
    c. achieving a flexible work role.
    d. all of the above.

22. The primary reason for women's lack of occupational success compared to men is
    a. interruptions in career advancement.
    b. job discrimination.
    c. differences in occupation.
    d. inability to handle responsibility.

173

_B_ 23. Which of the following statements is *not* true?
   a. Working women tend to score higher on measures of psychological well-being.
   b. Homemakers exhibit more marital satisfaction than employed women.
   c. Employed and nonemployed women do not differ in susceptibility to depression.
   d. Women's psychological adjustment is less affected by occupational prestige than men's.

_C_ 24. Which of the following statements is *not* true?
   a. Technological changes often make the jobs of middle-aged workers obsolete.
   b. Employers tend to discriminate against older job seekers.
   c. Middle-aged workers are increasingly unwilling to undergo retraining.
   d. People who change careers tend to be interested in the social-psychological aspects of jobs.

_C_ 25. Bicycle riding is an example of which of the following forms of leisure?
   a. relaxation
   b. diversion
   c. developmental pleasures
   d. creative pleasures

Matching

A. Styles of grandparenting:

_D_ 1. Formal
_C_ 2. Fun-seeker
_A_ 3. Surrogate-parent
_E_ 4. Reservoir of family wisdom
_B_ 5. Distant figure

a. Grandparent assumes child care responsibilities while parents work.
b. Grandparent has little consistent relationship with grandchild.
c. Grandparent expects mutually gratifying experiences with grandchild.
d. Grandparent occasionally provides special gifts or services.
e. Grandparent adopts authoritarian role in the family.

B. Styles of complementary relationships in marriage:

_B_ 1. Ibsenian
_D_ 2. Thurberian
_C_ 3. Master-servant girl
_A_ 4. Mother-son

a. Submissive, receptive male; dominant, nurturant female.
b. Dominant, nurturant male; submissive, receptive female.
c. Dominant, receptive male; submissive, nurturant female.
d. Nurturant, submissive male; dominant, receptive female.

174

C. Basic types of marriages:

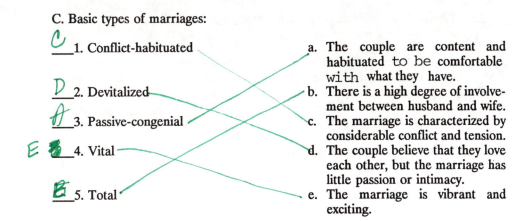

_C_ 1. Conflict-habituated

a. The couple are content and habituated to be comfortable with what they have.

_D_ 2. Devitalized

b. There is a high degree of involvement between husband and wife.

_A_ 3. Passive-congenial

c. The marriage is characterized by considerable conflict and tension.

E _d_ 4. Vital

d. The couple believe that they love each other, but the marriage has little passion or intimacy.

_B_ 5. Total

e. The marriage is vibrant and exciting.

ANSWERS

True or False

1. F
2. F
3. F
4. T
5. T
6. T
7. F
8. F
9. T
10. T
11. F
12. T
13. F
14. F
15. T
16. F
17. T
18. T
19. F
20. T
21. T
22. F
23. T
24. F
25. F

Sentence Completion

1. mentor relationships
2. half
3. bidirectional
4. high
5. link
6. inner conflicts
7. equals
8. leisure-time activity
9. less
10. reversal
11. emotional support, advice
12. surrogate-parent
13. upturn
14. similarity, complementarity
15. conflict-habituated
16. passive-congenial
17. socially conditioned
18. growth
19. marriage
20. 90,000
21. more, less
22. nearly double
23. stability
24. job obsolescence, unemployment, age discrimination
25. relaxation

<u>Multiple Choice</u>

1. b
2. b
3. c
4. c
5. d
6. d
7. c
8. a
9. b
10. c
11. a
12. d
13. a
14. b
15. b
16. d
17. d
18. c
19. b
20. a
21. d
22. a
23. b
24. c
25. c

<u>Matching</u>

A. 1. d
   2. c
   3. a
   4. e
   5. b

B. 1. b
   2. d
   3. c
   4. a

C. 1. c
   2. d
   3. a
   4. e
   5. b

Chapter 15

LATE ADULTHOOD: PHYSICAL, COGNITIVE, AND PERSONALITY DEVELOPMENT

CHAPTER OUTLINE

SUMMARY OF KEY CONCEPTS

1. In old age people undergo numerous physical, cognitive, and socioemotional changes. The overall experience of growing older may be affected by the negative consequences of *ageism*.

2. The term *senescence* refers to *primary aging*, or the normal age-related changes that occur in response to biological decline. These changes include changes in physical appearance such as wrinkles and graying of hair. The major systems of the body, such as the cardiovascular and pulmonary systems, continue to

decline in efficiency. There is an acceleration in sensory decline, particularly in hearing. Regular, moderate physical activity can help slow the aging process.

3. Old people are more susceptible to disease and less likely to recover quickly. In old age people are also more likely to suffer from such mental disorders as depression, chronic anxiety, and hypochondriasis. Older white males have the highest suicide rate of any group.

4. *Dementia* is a common condition in old age and involves declines in physical, cognitive, and personality behaviors as a result of brain deterioration or damage. Alzheimer's disease, the most common dementia, is a chronic and progressive disorder that can last for fifteen years or more before the victim dies.

5. The aging process cannot be satisfactorily explained by a single theory. It has been explained as resulting from an accumulation of errors at the cellular level, as due to wear and tear on the body over the years, or as caused by inadequate delivery of nutrients to the cells. Research has shown a definite link between heredity and longevity.

6. Certain aspects of intelligence seem to decline with age. They include psycho-motor skills, attention, memory, and inductive reasoning. Social knowledge, verbal-conceptual ability, and arithmetic reasoning are not affected by age.

7. Many factors affect the ability of older people to perform well on intelligence tests. Among them are the pacing of the problems, the degree of arousal of the autonomic nervous system, and motivation.

8. According to Erikson, the crisis faced by older people is that of *ego integrity versus despair*. Most old people continue to grow psychologically. Old people must adjust to retirement, physical aging, and the inevitability of death.

9. There are two opposing theories regarding the best means of adapting to old age. The *disengagement theory* suggests that old people can adjust best by reducing their involvement with other people and becoming more interested in themselves. According to the *activity theory*, activity and involvement in others keep a person healthy and youthful.

KEY TERMS AND PHRASES

ageism
senescence
primary aging
secondary aging
osteoporosis
hypokinetic disease
functional disorders
organic brain syndromes
dementia
multi-infarct dementia

divided attention
selective attention
primary memory
secondary memory
competence
performance
ego integrity vs. despair
life review
interiority
disengagement theory
activity theory

REVIEW QUESTIONS

1. What is meant by ageism?

2. Distinguish between primary and secondary aging.

3. What changes in sensory and organic functioning occur with age?

4. What can be done to reduce the physical effects of aging?

5. What types of mental disorder occur most frequently in older people?

6. Briefly describe the theories that have been proposed to explain the aging process.

7. How is intellectual functioning affected by age, if at all?

8. Why do the elderly tend to score lower than younger adults on intelligence tests?

9. What are the primary developmental tasks of late adulthood?

10. Briefly describe the two main theories of social interaction and adjustment in old age.

EXERCISES

1. Briefly describe the following stages of aging.

THEORY	DESCRIPTION
Cellular error	
Wear and tear	
Stress theory	
Deprivation	
Metabolic waste	
Immunological	
Autoimmune	

2. Identify the developmental tasks of late adulthood outlined by Erikson and Peck.

ERIKSON	PECK

QUIZ

<u>True or False</u>

F 1. The term *ageism* refers to inability to cope with the inevitable changes that occur as a person grows older.

T 2. People over the age of 65 constitute the fastest-growing segment of the U.S. population.

F 3. Gradual loss of neural tissue and slowing of central-nervous-system activity are examples of secondary aging.

F 4. Osteoporosis is a consequence of aging that cannot be prevented.

T 5. The most common disability of the aged eye is cataracts.

T 6. Losses in cardiac output begin in early adulthood.

F 7. Because of the slowing of neural responses, elderly people are unable to perform rapid, finely coordinated movements.

F 8. The term *hypokinetic disease* refers to the postural stoop that develops during the aging process.

T 9. Organic brain syndromes have a biological cause.

F 10. Depression is relatively rare among elderly people.

T 11. Alzheimer's disease is irreversible.

F 12. The theory of cellular error compares the human organism to a machine and human cells to machine parts.

T 13. The autoimmune theory states that as the immune system deteriorates, the body destroys both normal and abnormal cells.

T 14. Longitudinal studies indicate that most intellectual functions are stable through the fifth decade.

F 15. The saying "You can't teach an old dog new tricks" accurately reflects the learning performance of older adults.

T 16. The term *divided attention* refers to the ability to process more than one source of information simultaneously.

F 17. Primary memory is equivalent to long-term memory.

F 18. It has been hypothesized that the earliest abilities to emerge in development are also the first to disappear during aging.

T 19. Researchers have found that as people age they become increasingly field-dependent.

F 20. Verbal conceptual ability tends to decline with age.

T 21. Some psychologists suggest that the decreased performance of the elderly does not necessarily indicate decreased competence.

_T_ 22. Late adulthood is a time of continued psychological growth.

_F_ 23. Most theorists believe that older people should concentrate on the physical changes they are undergoing, rather than focusing on mental activities.

_F_ 24. Gender-typed qualities tend to increase with age.

_T_ 25. According to disengagement theory, a high level of role activity is associated with low morale in elderly people.

Sentence Completion

1. _Ageism_ refers to any situation in which people are negatively judged on the basis of age.

2. It is estimated that the over-65 population will _more than double_ by the middle of the twenty-first century.

3. The acceleration of senescence by extrinsic factors is referred to as _secondary aging_

4. One of the most pronounced changes in physical appearance during the aging years is _postural_ stoop.

5. The most usual sensory loss associated with aging is _hearing_.

6. Aging is accompanied by reductions in the _efficiency_ and _ease_ with which the body's organs function.

7. After the age of 30, between _20,000_ and _100,000_ nerve cells die each day.

8. It is primarily when older people have to _change the direction_ their movement in response to new information that impairment occurs.

9. The most common chronic conditions restricting activity in individuals 65 and over are _heart disease, hypertension,_ and _arthritis, visual impairment orthopedic problems?_

10. The term _hypokinetic disease_ refers to loss of function due to inactivity.

11. The best way to keep physically fit in late adulthood is to begin a program of _exercise_ in early or middle adulthood.

12. The most frequent functional disorders in the elderly are _depressive reaction_

13. In _Alzheimers_ a progressive and irreversible deterioration of the brain tissue results in increasing deterioration in mental, social, and personality behaviors.

14. _Multi-infarct_ dementia is believed to be caused by mini-strokes brought on by arteriosclerosis.

15. The *Deprivation* theory of aging holds that aging is due to the inadequate delivery of essential nutrients and oxygen to cells.

16. According to the *autoimmune* theory of aging, as the immune system deteriorates, the body cannot tell the difference between normal and abnormal cells and therefore destroys both.

17. By far the most frequently studies component of intellectual functioning in the aged is their performance on *std. IQ test*.

18. Research on the elderly suggests that there are age-related *decrements* in the ability to acquire and remember information.

19. *Selective attention* refers to the ability to attend to relevant information while ignoring irrelevant information.

20. Most research suggests that *primary* memory capacity does not usually decline with age.

21. Researchers have found that as people age they become increasingly field-*dependent*

22. Cognitive deficits in the elderly have been linked to *neurological* intactness and level of *social* interaction.

23. According to Erikson, during old age the individual experiences the crisis of *ego integrity* versus *despair*.

24. According to Peck, older people must come to grips with *retirement*, *physical decline*, and *mortality*.

25. According to Gutmann, during the aging process men gradually shift from an *active mastery* approach to the world to a *passive-accomodative* approach, while women show the opposite trend.

Multiple Choice

B 1. The term *ageism* refers to
   a. the tendency to identify with a particular age.
   b. situations in which people are negatively judged on the basis of age.
   c. the decline in intelligence that occurs with age.
   d. the study of the aging process.

C 2. By the mid-twenty-first century the population of people over 65 is expected to
   a. decrease dramatically.
   b. increase slightly.
   c. more than double.
   d. remain approximately the same.

_D_3. Physical deterioration due to grief at the loss of a spouse is an example of
   a. senescence.
   b. obsolescence.
   c. primary aging.
   d. secondary aging.

_A_4. The so-called dowager's hump is due to
   a. osteoporosis.
   b. postural stoop.
   c. spinal disc compression.
   d. none of the above.

_D_5. Elderly people are likely to suffer from
   a. decreased night vision.
   b. cataracts.
   c. glaucoma.
   d. all of the above.

_C_6. Which of the following statements is *not* true?
   a. The cardiovascular system deteriorates significantly with age.
   b. Shortness of breath is common among older people.
   c. There is little change in neurological function in old age.
   d. Older people are more susceptible to disease than younger people.

_A_7. Older people are especially troubled by
   a. inability to care for themselves.
   b. restrictions on their activities.
   c. pain caused by chronic conditions.
   d. the fear of dying from an illness.

_B_8. Hypokinetic disease refers to
   a. secondary aging due to stress.
   b. loss of function due to inactivity.
   c. the slowing down of the central nervous system.
   d. sensory changes in late adulthood.

_B_9. Mental disorders for which there is no apparent biological basis are known as
   a. organic brain syndromes.
   b. functional disorders.
   c. dementias.
   d. none of the above.

_C_10. A condition in which a person suffers a series of strokes over a long period is known as
   a. Alzheimer's disease.
   b. hypokinetic disease.
   c. multi-infarct dementia.
   d. Down syndrome.

D 11. A theory in which aging is attributed to the slow poisoning of the body by itself is the
    a. cellular-error theory.
    b. wear-and-tear theory.
    c. stress theory.
    d. metabolic-waste theory.

A 12. According to the deprivation theory, aging is due to
    a. inadequate delivery of essential nutrients and oxygen to cells.
    b. the accumulation of errors in the transfer of information at the cellular level.
    c. the wearing out of human cells as a result of prolonged use.
    d. the reduction of the energy capacities of the organism as a result of stressful life events.

C 13. The range of intellectual performance a person displays under different environmental conditions is known as
    a. crystallized intelligence.
    b. fluid intelligence.
    c. intellectual plasticity.
    d. intellectual complexity.

A 14. Being able to engage in a conversation and watch television at the same time is an example of
    a. divided attention.
    b. selective attention.
    c. an attention deficit.
    d. an information-processing deficit.

D 15. Which of the following statements is *not* true?
    a. Learning in the elderly is adversely affected by fast-paced conditions. T
    b. When elderly adults are allowed to pace themselves, their performance improves. T
    c. The performance of the elderly under self-paced conditions does not equal that of younger adults. T
    d. Learning that occurs at a slow pace eliminates the performance difference between younger and older adults. NOT TRUE

A 16. Which of the following does not usually decline with age?
    a. primary memory
    b. secondary memory
    c. long-term memory
    d. encoded memory

B 17. Which of the following statements is *not* true?
- a. Older adults do not perform well on tests of advanced concepts. T
- b. Older adults outperform middle-aged adults on tests of classification ability.
- c. Consistent performance decrements for the elderly have been found in the area of formal operations.
- d. Institutionalized adults perform less well on cognitive tests than adults living in the community.

C 18. When given a series of objects to sort, older adults are likely to group them according to
- a. perceptual similarity.
- b. categorical criteria.
- c. thematic criteria.
- d. none of the above.

D 19. The lower levels of intellectual performance among older adults may be due to
- a. generational and social changes.
- b. health-related factors.
- c. limited contact with other people.
- d. all of the above.

B 20. According to Erikson, during old age the individual experiences the crisis of ego integrity versus
- a. isolation.
- b. despair.
- c. stagnation.
- d. identity confusion.

D 21. The term *life review* refers to
- a. finding personal satisfaction beyond the work activities that have been important for self-definition in earlier periods.
- b. shifting values away from the physical domain to the domain of interpersonal relations.
- c. accepting the inevitability of death.
- d. organizing memories and reinterpreting earlier actions and decisions.

C 22. Which of the following statements is *not* true?
- a. All theories of development in old age emphasize the challenges posed by declining health.
- b. Generativity is important in the final years of life as well as in middle adulthood.
- c. Older people function better if they ignore the fact of mortality.
- d. The developmental tasks of old age are related to earlier developmental tasks.

D 23. Which of the following statements is true?
  a. People over 65 usually define themselves as old. F
  b. A man is considered "old" earlier than a woman. F
  c. Social policies attempt to ignore widely held definitions of old age. F
  d. None of the above.

A 24. According to Gutmann, an active-mastery approach to the world is characteristic of
  a. younger men.
  b. older men.
  c. younger women.
  d. all of the above.

B 25. Which of the following proposes a lifestyle in which elderly people maintain their previous levels of social interaction and involvement in the world?
  a. disengagement theory
  b. activity theory
  c. interiority theory
  d. hypokinetic theory

Matching

A. Theories of aging:

C 1. Cellular error

D 2. Wear and tear

A 3. Stress theory

F 4. Deprivation

G 5. Metabolic waste

E 6. Immunological theory

B 7. Autoimmune theory

a. Stressful life events reduce the energy capacities of the organism.
b. As the immune system deteriorates the body destroys both normal and abnormal cells.
c. Aging results from accumulated errors in the transfer of information at the cellular level.
d. Human cells wear out with prolonged use.
e. The immune system deteriorates and cannot provide protection from foreign substances.
f. Aging is due to inadequate delivery of nutrients and oxygen to cells.
g. The gradual buildup of waste products of metabolism interferes with cell functioning.

B. Aspects of information processing:

D 1. Divided attention

a. Ability to attend to relevant information while ignoring irrelevant information.

187

_A_ 2. Selective attention

_B_ 3. Primary memory

_C_ 4. Secondary memory

b. Recall of information that is still being attended to.

c. Encoding of information that is no longer the focus of active or selective attention.

d. Ability to process more than one source of information simultaneously.

ANSWERS

True or False

1. F
2. T
3. F
4. F
5. T
6. T
7. F
8. F
9. T
10. F
11. T
12. F
13. T
14. T
15. F
16. T
16. T
17. F
18. F
19. T
20. F
21. T
22. T
23. F
24. F
25. T

Sentence Completion

1. ageism
2. more than double
3. secondary aging
4. postural
5. hearing
6. efficiency, ease
7. 20,000, 100,000
8. change the direction of
9. heart disease, arthritis, hypertension, visual impairments, orthopedic problems
10. hypokinetic disease
11. exercise
12. depressive reactions
13. Alzheimer's disease
14. multi-infarct
15. deprivation
16. autoimmune
17. standard IQ tests
18. decrements
19. selective attention
20. primary
21. dependent
22. neurological, social
23. integrity, despair
24. retirement, physical decline, mortality
25. active-mastery, passive-accommodative

Multiple Choice

1. b
2. c
3. d
4. a
5. d
6. c
7. a
8. b
9. b
10. c
11. d
12. a

13. c
14. a
15. d
16. a
17. b
18. c
19. d
20. b
21. d
22. c
23. d
24. a
25. b

Matching

A. 1. c
    2. d
    3. a
    4. f
    5. g
    6. e
    7. b

B. 1. d
    2. a
    3. b
    4. c

Chapter 16

LATE ADULTHOOD:
FAMILY LIFE, SOCIAL RELATIONS, AND RETIREMENT

CHAPTER OUTLINE

SUMMARY OF KEY CONCEPTS

1. Many adjustments to aging must be made within the contexts of family and social relations and work. Important influences include retirement, accommodating to a reduced income, and the death of a spouse.

2. Although poverty and illness may create strains, research indicates that the quality of married life in old age is good. People who have a spouse to buffer them against the stresses of old age live longer and experience less mental illness and loneliness.

3. Older people enjoy sex but are often frustrated by the lack of an available and willing partner. Older people focus less on sexual performance and more on sexual pleasure.

4. Most older people live independently of their children, often nearby. They rely on them in times of illness, but also give advice, emotional support, and services.

5. Relationships with grandchildren vary considerably. Research suggests that older adults and their adolescent and young-adult grandchildren influence one another in some areas.

6. Widowhood represents the single greatest loss suffered by aging individuals. Most widows prefer to maintain their independence despite the problem of loneliness.

7. Only about 5 percent of older people live in nursing homes, but about 20 percent will spend some time in an extended-care facility. Generally, people enter an institution when their physical condition is deteriorating and no other care is available. Alternatives to institutionalization include age-segregated residential communities, in-home care, and apartments near the home of an adult child.

8. People who choose to retire usually do so because of adequate financial resources, good pension plans, desire to spend more time with family, or dislike of their job. Involuntary retirement is associated with mandatory retirement policies and poor health.

9. During retirement individuals develop, implement, reevaluate, and enact their plans for the retirement years. Some adults find retirement exciting, while others are disenchanted.

10. Leisure activities in old age are mostly confined to sedentary activities. People who are actively involved in leisure pursuits are usually more satisfied with their postretirement life.

KEY TERMS AND PHRASES

social integration
isolation

REVIEW QUESTIONS

1. What factors determine love and marital satisfaction in old age?

2. How does aging affect sexual interest and activity?

3. Briefly describe the changes that take place in people's relations with their adult children and grandchildren as they age.

4. What special problems are faced by widows?

5. What proportion of older people are institutionalized? What factors lead to residence in an institution?

6. Briefly describe the theories that have been proposed to explain the social relations of older people.

7. How do older people generally relate to siblings and friends?

8. What factors contribute to the decision to retire?

9. Briefly describe the process of retirement.

10. What factors influence people's attitudes toward retirement?

EXERCISES

1. Compare and contrast the two main social theories of aging, including the advantages and disadvantages of each.

THEORY	DESCRIPTION	ADVANTAGES/DISADVANTAGES
Disengagement		
Activity		

2. Name and describe Atchley's seven phases of retirement.

	PHASE	DESCRIPTION
1		

2
_____

3
_____

4
_____

5
_____

6
_____

7
_____

QUIZ

<u>True or False</u>

_T_1. For married adults, the last stage in the family life cycle is usually ten to fifteen years long.

_F_2. Most elderly couples are unhappy, lonely, and isolated from each other and from their families.

_T_3. Elderly people tend to experience <u>less disruption in their lives</u> than younger people do.

_F_4. The amount of love expressed in a marriage tends to increase over time.

_T_5. Gender-role reversal appears to contribute to the success of late marriages.

_T_6. Many people enjoy sex well into old age.

_T_7. Contrary to popular belief, <u>hormonal changes do not affect sexual functioning in old age.</u>

_T_8. The majority of elderly people prefer to live independently of their family.

_F_9. More older people receive help from their children than give help to them.

_F_10. Grandparents have a strong influence on the sexual and religious values of their adolescent grandchildren.

_F_ 11. About one-third of the population of adults over 65 have never married.

_T_ 12. Older men are much more likely to remarry following the death of their spouse than older women are.

_F_ 13. Older people prefer residence in a nursing home over life in a family or home environment.

_F_ 14. A "granny flat" is a specially designed apartment for handicapped elderly people.

_T_ 15. Activity theory suggests that satisfactory aging requires that the individual continue to be involved in social roles and relationships.

_T_ 16. People who choose to withdraw from social roles are more likely to feel satisfied with their life situation than those who are forced to do so.

_F_ 17. Most elderly people are estranged from their siblings.

_T_ 18. Friendships can help compensate for the personal and social losses experienced by elderly people.

_F_ 19. Most workers welcome retirement as a chance to escape from hard work and do things they have always wanted to do.

_F_ 20. Under the social security system, self-employed people must retire at age 75.

_T_ 21. The major factors leading to early retirement are financial status and health.

_T_ 22. In Atchley's scheme, the first phase of retirement is the remote phase.

_F_ 23. Atchley's final phase of retirement is the stability phase.

_T_ 24. High morale during retirement depends on an adequate retirement income.

_T_ 25. Most of the leisure activities of retired people can be engaged in alone.

Sentence Completion

1. The last stage in the family life cycle is described as the time from _____ to the _____ of both husband and wife.

2. Most couples who enter late adulthood together feel especially _____.

3. The two factors that give the older marriage its unique character are the gradual shift in focus away from the _____ and the _____ of the husband (and more recently the wife).

4. Couples who have not shared _____ throughout their marriage enjoy a less satisfactory relationship in later life.

5. One factor that may help explain the success of some late marriages is the _____ that characterizes some older couples.

6. Masters and Johnson found that people who maintained an active sexual life during early stages of life were _____ likely to continue to be sexually active in later life.

7. Sexuality in old age is complicated by _____ problems.

8. The majority of older people prefer to live _____.

9. Older people rely primarily on their children in times of _____.

10. The morale of grandparents is _____ to the amount of contact they have with their grandchildren.

11. _____ represents the greatest emotional and social loss suffered by individuals in the normal course of the lifespan.

12. The gender difference in widowhood represents a higher _____ rate for men than women and the fact that older men are much more likely to _____ than older women.

13. The average nursing-home resident is approximately _____ years old, _____, and _____.

14. Institutionalization is most likely to occur when the person's _____ condition shows evidence of increased deterioration.

15. In the future the need for more _____ living arrangements for the elderly is likely to become an even more important issue.

16. _____ versus _____ refers to the degree of interpersonal activity and organizational participation that an individual engages in.

17. Frequency of social participation is a _____ predictor of morale among older adults.

18. Relationships with _____ play an important role in the life of the aging adult.

19. Older men report more _____ friendships than older women do.

20. Retirement age is often described as an artifact of the _____ system.

21. _____ people are not affected by mandatory retirement.

22. The major factors in deciding on early retirement are _____ and _____.

23. The transition from worker to nonworker has been labeled the _____ phase.

24. The main factor influencing people's attitudes toward retirement is the amount of _____ they have.

25. Contrary to popular opinion, _____ does not deteriorate after retirement.

Multiple Choice

B 1. Which of the following statements is *not* true?
   a. The last stage of the family life cycle is usually ten to fifteen years long. T
   (b.) The period from retirement to death tends to be longer for men than for women.
   c. Historically, the final stage of the family life cycle is a relatively new phenomenon. T
   d. Older married couples often describe this time as the happiest period of their marriage. T

D 2. According to older couples, the most satisfying aspect of their relationship is
   a. respect.
   b. sexual intimacy.
   c. communication.
   (d.) emotional security.

7. **B** 3. In later life, the amount of love expressed in a marriage tends to
   a. decline.
   b. increase.
   c. fluctuate dramatically.
   d. remain the same as in earlier years.

D 4. Compared to the unmarried elderly, married older people are likely to
   a. live longer.
   b. experience less mental illness.
   c. be less lonely.
   (d.) all of the above.

A 5. Which of the following statements is *not* true?
   a. Older adults are not very interested in sexual pleasures.
   b. Frequency of sexual intercourse declines with age. T
   c. People who were sexually active in early adulthood tend to remain so in later life. T
   d. The form of sexual activity changes in old age. T

A 6. What percentage of elderly people live with their children?
   - a. under 15 percent
   - b. about 25 percent
   - c. 50 percent
   - d. 65 percent

C 7. The relationship between older people and their children tends to be characterized by
   - a. considerable dependence by parents on their adult children.
   - b. financial dependence of the children on their aging parents.
   - c. mutual assistance.
   - d. minimal interaction.

C 8. Grandparents are most likely to influence their adolescent grandchildren in the area of
   - a. sexuality.
   - b. religion.
   - c. career plans.
   - d. none of the above.

B 9. What proportion of adults over age 65 have never married?
   - a. 1 percent
   - b. 5 percent
   - c. 10 percent
   - d. 25 percent

D 10. Which of the following statements is *not* true?
   - a. One-half of women in the United States over age 65 are widowed. T
   - b. Older men are much more likely to remarry than older women. T
   - c. Widowhood requires establishing a new relationship with society. T
   - d. Most widows prefer to live with their married children.

D 11. Which of the following statements is true?
   - a. Women are more likely than men to remarry following the death of their spouse. F
   - b. Widowers are less well off financially than widows. F
   - c. Women generally suffer more than men following the loss of a spouse. F
   - d. None of the above.

A 12. The average nursing home resident is
   - a. female.
   - b. about 70 years old.
   - c. black.
   - d. all of the above.

D 13. Compared to older people who are not institutionalized, nursing home residents
    a.   are more dependent.
    b.   have fewer friends.
    c.   are better off economically.
    d.   none of the above.

A 14. Residents of specialized housing for the elderly
    a.   enjoy participating in social activities.
    b.   face higher living costs.
    c.   become cut off from younger people.
    d.   all of the above.

B 15. The degree of interpersonal activity that a person engages in is referred to as
    a.   generativity.
    b.   social integration.
    c.   interiority.
    d.   social adjustment.

B 16. Which of the following is *not* a useful predictor of life satisfaction and morale among older adults?
    a.   whether social withdrawal is voluntary or involuntary
    b.   frequency of social participation
    c.   the subjective meaning of social integration
    d.   the quality of a person's social relations

C 17. Which of the following statements is *not* true?
    a.   Most older people have living brothers and sisters. T
    b.   Relationships with siblings are important in the life of the aging adult. T
    c.   Male siblings are especially effective in preserving family relationships. F
    d.   For aged women, the presence of sisters results in greater concern about social relationships outside of the family. T

C 18. Which of the following statements is true?
    a.   Older men have fewer friends than older women do. F
    b.   Older women spend less time with their friends than older men do. F
    c.   Older men reveal less about themselves to their friends than older women do. T
    d.   Older women report more cross-gender friendship than older men do. F

A 19. Which of the following are more likely to retire by choice?
    a.   people with adequate financial resources
    b.   black workers
    c.   people from lower socioeconomic groups
    d.   people who are in poor health

_C_ 20. What proportion of adults work after retirement?
   a. almost all
   b. about half
   c. over 10 percent
   d. very few

_B_ 21. The average age at retirement in major industries is
   a. 55.
   b. 58.
   c. 65.
   d. 70.

_B_ 22. According to Atchley, which phase of the retirement process is characterized by feelings of excitement and even euphoria?
   a. the near preretirement phase
   b. the honeymoon phase
   d. the reorientation phase
   d. the stability phase

_D_ 23. During which phase of the retirement process does the individual decide on long-term goals?
   a. the remote phase
   b. the honeymoon phase
   c. the disenchantment phase
   d. the reorientation phase

_B_ 24. Which of the following are most likely to have difficulty adjusting to retirement?
   a. unskilled workers
   b. satisfied workers
   c. white-collar workers
   d. workers with adequate savings

_D_ 25. Retirement represents the loss of
   a. a social role.
   b. social contacts.
   c. power and prestige.
   d. all of the above.

Matching

Phases of the retirement process:

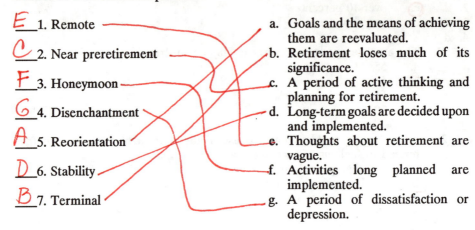

E 1. Remote

C 2. Near preretirement

F 3. Honeymoon

G 4. Disenchantment

A 5. Reorientation

D 6. Stability

B 7. Terminal

a. Goals and the means of achieving them are reevaluated.

b. Retirement loses much of its significance.

c. A period of active thinking and planning for retirement.

d. Long-term goals are decided upon and implemented.

e. Thoughts about retirement are vague.

f. Activities long planned are implemented.

g. A period of dissatisfaction or depression.

ANSWERS

True or False

1. T
2. F
3. T
4. F
5. T
6. T
7. F
8. T
9. F
10. F
11. F
12. T
13. F
14. F
15. T
16. T
17. F
18. T
19. F
20. F
21. T
22. T
23. F
24. T
25. T

Sentence Completion

1. retirement, death
2. fortunate
3. children, retirement
4. domestic duties
5. gender role reversal
6. more
7. medical
8. independently
9. illness
10. unrelated
11. widowhood
12. mortality, remarry
13. 80, white, female
14. physical
15. flexible
16. social integration, isolation
17. poor
18. siblings
19. cross-gender
20. social security
21. self-employed
22. financial status, health
23. honeymoon
24. choice
25. health

Multiple Choice

1. b
2. d
3. c
4. d
5. a
6. a
7. c
8. c
9. b
10. d
11. d
12. a
13. d
14. a
15. b
16. b
17. c
18. c
19. a
20. c
21. a
22. b
23. d
24. b
25. d

Matching

1. e
2. c
3. f
4. g
5. a
6. d
7. b

Chapter 17

THE FINAL STAGE OF LIFE:
DEATH, DYING, AND BEREAVEMENT

CHAPTER OUTLINE

SUMMARY OF KEY CONCEPTS

1. Death is the final stage of the life cycle. The determination of death has become more complex as a result of advances in medical technology.

2. Death can occur at any point in the lifespan, but the nature of death varies with age. Accidents and birth defects are more common in early childhood; in adolescence and young adulthood death by violent means occurs more frequently. During middle adulthood people die from disease and accidents.

3. The impact of death varies with age and cognitive ability. By the age of ten months infants have formed attachments and are capable of experiencing loss and separation. When separation is not temporary, as in the death of a parent, the child may continue to feel anxious in later life.

4. Preschool children define all things that move as alive. Death is seen as reversible and similar to sleep. By age 6 death is no longer seen as reversible but is not yet seen as inevitable. At age 9 or 10 the child has an adult concept of death; life and death are seen as internal processes that belong to all living things.

5. Although adolescents appear to have an adult understanding of death, they view it as distant or remote from their experience. In young adulthood, marriage and parenthood help define a person's view of death.

6. Concern with death peaks during middle adulthood as people become aware of their physical limitations and experience the death of their parents. In late adulthood death becomes a realistic concern as the elderly accept death as a natural part of living.

7. Some people experience a *terminal drop* in cognitive and intellectual skills just before dying. Others experience isolation and loneliness as their spouse and peers die.

8. Kübler-Ross describes stages of adjustment that dying people experience: denial, anger, bargaining, depression, and acceptance. Other researchers suggest that each person has a unique dying trajectory that influences the speed with which he or she dies.

9. *Hospice* care has been developed to help people through the dying process. Some individuals make out living wills to ensure that no extraordinary medical efforts will be used to prolong their life.

10. *Bereavement* is a condition of loss during which people grieve and mourn the death of a loved one. *Mourning* practices differ in different cultures, but the experience of *grief* is believed to be universal.

11. People go through three stages in the experience of grief: numbness, yearning, and protest; disorganization and depression; and recovery. Children experience emotional reactions similar to those of adults, but they lack the cognitive ability and life experiences to help them understand their own reactions.

KEY TERMS AND PHRASES

terminal stage of life
terminal drop
hospice
euthanasia
bereavement

grief
mourning
living will

REVIEW QUESTIONS

1. How do the causes of death vary across the lifespan?

2. How do conceptions of death differ during different stages of life?

3. What is meant by the terminal stage of life?

4. List Kübler-Ross's five stages of dying.

5. In what ways has Kübler-Ross's theory been criticized?

6. What is hospice care?

7. Briefly describe the concepts of euthanasia and the living will.

8. Distinguish among bereavement, grief, and mourning.

9. What are the symptoms of grief? What are the stages of grief?

10. How does bereavement affect children and adolescents?

EXERCISES

1. Briefly summarize conceptions of death from infancy to late adulthood.

AGE GROUP	CONCEPTION OF DEATH
Infancy	

Early childhood	
Middle childhood	
Adolescence and youth	
Early adulthood	
Middle adulthood	
Late adulthood	

2. Describe Kübler-Ross's five stages of the dying process.

STAGE	DESCRIPTION
1	
2	
3	
4	
5	

QUIZ

<u>True or False</u>

____1. The psychology of death has been studied intensively for over a century.

____2. Death is said to occur at the moment that the heart stops beating.

____3. It is possible for death to occur before birth.

____4. Chronological age influences a person's expectations of death.

____5. Infants comprehend the concept of death by the time they reach their first birthday.

____6. Preschool children see death as a reversible process.

____7. By age 6 children realize that death is inevitable.

____8. Children achieve an adult concept of death at about age 10.

____9. Most adolescents do not have a sense of longevity.

____10. Concern with death reaches its peak in early adulthood.

____11. Most elderly people do not fear death.

____12. The term *terminal drop* refers to the period in which a person is aware of his or her impending death.

____13. The psychological process of dying usually begins before the physiological process.

____14. According to Kübler-Ross, the first stage of the dying process is characterized by bargaining.

____15. The last stage of the dying process is acceptance.

____16. Critics have pointed out that Kübler-Ross's stages of dying are not universal.

____17. The hospice movement arose out of public concern about artificial prolongation of life.

____18. Euthanasia refers to means by which people can express their wishes for the disposition of their own lives, should they later lose mental competence.

____19. The state or condition of loss is known as bereavement.

____20. Anticipatory mourning occurs in expectation of a person's death and consists of overt, culturally prescribed expressions of grief.

____21. The initial stage of grief is characterized by disorganization and depression.

____22. Recovery from grief depends on the ability to express emotions such as anger or guilt.

____23. It is more difficult for families to cope with an unexpected death than one for which they are prepared.

____24. Bereavement during adolescence may interfere with the formation of an adult identity.

____25. Most people who die in adolescence are victims of serious diseases.

Sentence Completion

1. Many physicians advocate a new medical and legal definition of death based on the death of the _____.

2. During childhood, death is more likely to occur from _____ or _____.

3. For infants, _____ is a powerful analogy to death.

4. During early childhood, life and death are _____ and _____ states.

5. The preoperational child regards death as similar to _____.

6. _____ of death is characteristic of children's conception of death during middle childhood.

7. Children who face terminal illness in middle childhood appear to _____ their predicament.

8. For young people, death is a _____ and _____ event.

9. Concern with death appears to peak during _____.

10. Fear of death in the elderly is associated with lack of _____.

11. The _____ stage of life is the time when people are aware of their impending death.

12. The _____ process of dying begins when the person learns that he or she has a fatal physical condition.

13. According to Kübler-Ross, the first stage of the dying process is characterized by _____ and _____.

14. A person who has accepted death appreciates _____ and _____.

15. In all stages of the dying process the patient persists in feeling _____.

16. Some researchers believe it is possible to project a dying _____ for each individual who approaches death.

17. The goal of the _____ movement is more humane treatment of the dying.

18. The word _____ means "inducing an easy and painless death for reasons assumed to be merciful."

19. _____ are documents by means of which people can express their wishes for the disposition of their own lives.

20. _____ is the emotional response to the loss of a significant person.

21. In _____, people grieve in expectation of a person's death.

22. In the first stage of grief the bereaved person experiences _____.

23. The impact of the death of a loved one on the family depends on the _____ and _____ of the family and the degree of _____ for the death.

24. Children lack the _____ and _____ that would enable them to cope effectively with bereavement.

25. Adolescents who face death feel _____ at lost opportunities and _____ about what to do with the time remaining to them.

Multiple Choice

___1.   Death and dying have been studied extensively
   a.   throughout human history.
   b.   since the time of the Industrial Revolution.
   c.   since the turn of the century.
   d.   only in recent decades.

___2.   Today death is usually defined as occurring when
   a.   the heart stops beating.
   b.   breathing stops.
   c.   brain activity ceases.
   d.   none of the above.

___3.   The most frequent cause of death in infants is
   a.   birth defects.
   b.   accidents.
   c.   illness.
   d.   homicide.

___4.   Most research on children's understanding of death suggests that children cannot comprehend death before the age of
   a.   10 months.
   b.   18 months.
   c.   2.
   d.   3.

___5.   Between the ages of 2 and 6, children ascribe the quality of life to anything that
   a.   moves.
   b.   is nearby.
   c.   breathes.
   d.   is a plant or animal.

___6. Before the age of 6, children consider death to be
    a. inevitable.
    b. reversible.
    c. normal.
    d. imminent.

___7. Children acquire an adult concept of death at about the age of
    a. 7.
    b. 10.
    c. 15.
    d. 18.

___8. The young adult's view of death is affected by
    a. marriage.
    b. pregnancy.
    c. childlessness.
    d. all of the above.

___9. Concern with death appears to peak in
    a. adolescence.
    b. youth.
    c. middle adulthood.
    d. late adulthood.

___10. The most common orientation toward death in people over 70 is
    a. extreme fear.
    b. denial.
    c. disbelief.
    d. acquiescence.

___11. People's scores on IQ tests tend to decline as they approach death. This phenomenon is known as
    a. the dying trajectory.
    b. terminal drop.
    c. psychological death.
    d. anticipatory grief.

___12. In Kübler-Ross's stages of dying, the initial stage is followed by a period of
    a. anger.
    b. bargaining.
    c. depression.
    d. acceptance.

___13. In Kübler-Ross's description of the dying process, the final stage is
    a. anger.
    b. depression.
    c. denial.
    d. acceptance.

_____14. Critics of Kübler-Ross's theory have pointed out that
   a.   the stages are not universal.
   b.   few patients express anger over dying.
   c.   the stages are rarely observed in men.
   d.   all of the above.

_____15. Which of the following statements is *not* true?
   a.   As people approach death, their physical condition deteriorates until
        the moment of actual death.
   b.   Relatives and friends of a dying person may make plans according
        to a predicted time for dying.
   c.   A person who is dying has little or no control over the time at which
        death will occur.
   d.   Most physicians believe it is important to communicate honestly with
        terminally ill patients.

_____16. The hospice movement is concerned with
   a.   more humane treatment of the dying.
   b.   making death easy and painless.
   c.   preventing the prolongation of life by artificial means.
   d.   improving communication between physicians and terminally ill
        patients.

_____17. Which of the following is sometimes referred to as "mercy killing"?
   a.   intensive care
   b.   hospice care
   c.   euthanasia
   d.   anesthesia

_____18. The purpose of a living will is to
   a.   induce an easy and painless death.
   b.   avoid artificial prolongation of life.
   c.   prevent anticipatory grief.
   d.   provide more humane treatment for the terminally ill.

_____19. The state or condition of loss is referred to as
   a.   bereavement.
   b.   grief.
   c.   mourning.
   d.   none of the above.

_____20. Which of the following is a common symptom of bereaved individuals?
   a.   somatic distress
   b.   shortness of breath
   c.   lack of muscular power
   d.   all of the above

____21. In the first stage of grief the bereaved person experiences
     a. yearning.
     b. numbness.
     c. protest.
     d. depression.

____22. The impact of death on family members depends on
     a. the family's emotional resources.
     b. the social supports available to the family.
     c. whether they are prepared for the death.
     d. all of the above.

____23. Which of the following statements is *not* true?
     a. Communication among family members aids in coping with bereavement.
     b. Families that deny the expression of emotions are better prepared to deal with grief.
     c. The most difficult death to cope with is the unexpected death.
     d. When a family member is terminally ill, family roles can be reorganized before the death.

____24. Which of the following statements is *not* true?
     a. Children who lose a parent have a greater-than-average tendency to suffer depression in adulthood.
     b. Children are able to experience bereavement before the age of 2.
     c. Adolescents lack the cognitive ability to deal effectively with bereavement.
     d. For young adults, bereavement amounts to a life-threatening condition.

____25. The most frequent cause of death in adolescence or youth is
     a. homicide.
     b. illness.
     c. accidents.
     d. combat.

Matching

A. Primary causes of death:

____1. Infancy

____2. Childhood
____3. Adolescence
____4. Early adulthood
____5. Late adulthood

     a. Motor-vehicle accidents, homicide, disease.
     b. Disease, suicide.
     c. Illness.
     d. Accidents, illness.
     e. Homicide, suicide, motor vehicle accidents.

B. Stages of the dying process:

___1
___2
___3
___4
___5

a. Bargaining
b. Denial and isolation
c. Depression
d. Anger
e. Acceptance

C. Stages of grief:

___1
___2
___3
___4

a. Recovery
b. Numbness
c. Disorganization and depression
d. Yearning and protest

ANSWERS

True or False

1. F
2. F
3. T
4. T
5. F
6. T
7. F
8. T
9. T
10. F
11. T
12. F
13. F
14. F
15. T
16. T
17. F
18. F
19. T
20. F
21. F
22. T
23. T
24. T
25. F

Sentence Completion

1. brain
2. accidents, illness
3. separation
4. temporary, reversible
5. sleep
6. personification
7. understand
8. distant, abstract
9. middle adulthood
10. ego integrity
11. terminal
12. psychological
13. denial, isolation
14. silence, constancy
15. hope
16. trajectory
17. hospice
18. euthanasia
19. living wills
20. grief
21. anticipatory grief
22. numbness
23. emotional, social, preparation
24. cognitive ability, life experiences
25. rage, uncertainty

Multiple Choice

1. d
2. c
3. a
4. c
5. a
6. b
7. b
8. d
9. c
10. d
11. b
12. a
13. d
14. a
15. c
16. a
17. c
18. b
19. a
20. d
21. b
22. d
23. b
24. c
25. c

Matching

A. 1. c
   2. d
   3. e
   4. a
   5. b

B. 1. b
   2. d
   3. a
   4. c
   5. e

C. 1. b
   2. d
   3. c
   4. a